ATD Soft Skills Series

Adaptability
in Talent
Development

Esther Jackson

PRESS

Alexandria, VA

ATD Press is an internationally renowned source of insightful and practical information on talent development, training, and professional development.

ATD Press
1640 King Street
Alexandria, VA 22314 USA

Ordering information: Books published by ATD Press can be purchased by visiting ATD's website at td.org/books or by calling 800.628.2783 or 703.683.8100.

Library of Congress Control Number: 2021939792

ISBN-10: 1-952157-51-X
ISBN-13: 978-1-952157-51-6
e-ISBN: 978-1-952157-52-3

ATD Press Editorial Staff
Director: Sarah Halgas
Manager: Melissa Jones
Content Manager, Career Development: Lisa Spinelli
Developmental Editor: Jack Harlow
Text Design: Shirley E.M. Raybuck
Cover Design: John Anderson

Printed by BR Printers, San Jose, CA

Contents

About the Series

The world of work is changing. As companies once prioritized radical workplace performance and productivity improvements, they focused on training their employees with the purpose of getting more work done faster. But companies have learned that while their people might be increasingly productive, they aren't working better, particularly with each other. Lurking on the horizon is always greater automation, which will continue to shift the balance between the needs for hard and soft skills. Employees of the future will spend more time on activities that machines are less capable of, such as managing people, applying expertise, and communicating with others. More than ever, soft skills are being recognized as a premium.

Enter talent development.

TD professionals play a unique role in addressing the increasing demand for soft skills. They work with people and on behalf of people: A trainer facilitating a group of learners. A team of instructional designers working cross-functionally to address a business need. A learning manager using influence to make the case for increased budget or resources. But how can TD professionals expect to develop future employees in these soft skills if they're not developing their own?

At the Association for Talent Development (ATD), we're dedicated to creating a world that works better and empowering TD professionals like you to develop talent in the workplace. As part of this effort, ATD developed the Talent Development Capability Model, a framework to guide the TD profession in what practitioners need to know and do to develop themselves, others, and their organizations. While soft skills appear most prominently under the Building Personal Capability domain, these crucial skills cross every capability in the model, including those under Developing Professional Capability and Impacting Organizational Capability. Soft skills enable TD professionals to take their instructional design, training delivery and facilitation, future readiness, change management, and other TD capabilities to the next level.

Just as TD professionals need resources on how to develop talent, they need guidance in improving their interpersonal and intrapersonal skills—to be more adaptable, self-aware and empathetic, creative, team-oriented and collaborative, and influential and persuasive. This ATD series provides such guidance.

Organized with two parts, each book in the ATD Soft Skills Series tackles one soft skill that TD professionals need to foster in themselves to help the people and organizations they serve. Part 1 breaks down the skill into what it is, why it's important, and the internal or external barriers to improving it. Part 2 turns the lens on the daily work of TD professionals and how they can practice and perfect that skill on the job. Featuring worksheets, self-reflection exercises, and best practices, these books will empower TD professionals to build career resiliency by matching their technical expertise with newfound soft skill abilities.

Books in the series:

- *Adaptability in Talent Development*
- *Emotional Intelligence in Talent Development*
- *Creativity in Talent Development*
- *Teamwork in Talent Development*
- *Influence in Talent Development*

We're happy to bring you the ATD Soft Skills Series and hope these books support you in your future learning and development.

Jack Harlow, Series Editor
Senior Developmental Editor, ATD Press

Series Foreword

Oh, Those Misnamed Soft Skills!

For years organizations have ignored soft skills and emphasized technical skills, often underestimating the value of working as a team, communicating effectively, using problem solving skills, and managing conflict. New managers have failed because their promotions are often based on technical qualifications rather than the soft skills that foster relationships and encourage teamwork. Trainers as recently as a dozen years ago were reluctant to say that they facilitated soft skills training. Why?

Soft Skills: The Past and Now

The reluctance to admit to delivering (or requiring) soft skills often starts with the unfortunate name, "soft," which causes people to view them as less valuable than "hard" skills such as accounting or engineering. The name suggests they are easy to master or too squishy to prioritize developing. On both counts that's wrong. They aren't. In fact, Seth Godin calls them "real" skills, as in, "Real because they work, because they're at the heart of what we need today" (Godin 2017).

Yet, as a society, we seem to value technical skills over interpersonal skills. We tend to admire the scientists who discovered the vaccine for COVID-19 over leaders who used their communication skills to engage the workforce when they were quarantined at home. We easily admit to not knowing how to fly an airplane but readily believe we are creative or can adapt on the fly. We think that because we've been listening all our lives, we are proficient at it—when we're not. As a result, we put much more emphasis on developing our technical skills through advanced degrees and post–higher education training or certifications to land that first or next job than we do on mastering our interpersonal and intrapersonal skills.

Fortunately, many businesses and their leaders are now recognizing the value of having a workforce that has technical knowledge supported by soft skills. That's good because soft skills matter more to your career than you may envision. Consider: as a part of the Jobs Reset Summit, the World Economic Forum determined that 50 percent of the workforce needed reskilling and upskilling. The summit also identified the top 10 job reskilling needs for the future. Eight of the 10 required skills in the 21st century are nontechnical; these skills include creativity, originality, and initiative; leadership and social influence; and resilience, stress tolerance, and flexibility (Whiting 2020). LinkedIn's 2019 *Global Talent Trends Report* showed that acquiring soft skills is the most important trend fueling the future of the workplace: 91 percent of the respondents said that soft skills matter as much or more than technical skills and 80 percent believed they were critical to organizational success (Chandler 2019). A Deloitte report (2017) suggested that "soft skill–intensive occupations will account for two-thirds of all jobs by 2030" and that employees who practice skills associated with collaboration, teamwork, and innovation may be worth $2,000 more per year to businesses. As the cost of robots decreases and AI improves, soft skills like teamwork, problem solving, creativity, and influence will become more important.

Soft skills may not be as optional as one might originally imagine.

Soft Skills: Their Importance

Soft skills are sometimes referred to as enterprise skills or employability skills. Despite their bad rap, they are particularly valuable because they are transferable between jobs, careers, departments, and even industries, unlike hard or technical skills, which are usually relevant only to specific jobs. Communication often lands at the top of the soft skill list, but the category encompasses other skills, such as those included in the ATD Soft Skills Series: emotional intelligence, adaptability, teamwork, creativity, and influence. These personal attributes influence how well employees build trust, establish accountability, and demonstrate professional ethics.

Soft skills are also important because almost every job requires employees to interact with others. Organizations require a workforce that has technical skills and formal qualifications for each job; however, the truth is that business is about relationships. And, organizations depend on relationships to be successful. This is where successful employees, productive organizations, and soft skills collide.

Soft Skills and the Talent Development Capability Model

Talent development professionals are essential links to ensure that organizations have all the technical and soft skills that are required for success. I sometimes get exhausted just thinking about everything we need to know to ensure success for our organizations, customers, leaders, learners, and ourselves. The TD profession is no cookie-cutter job. Every day is different; every design is different; every delivery is different; and every participant is different. We are lucky to have these differences because these broad requirements challenge us to grow and develop.

As TD professionals, we've always known that soft skills are critical for the workforce we're responsible for training and developing. But what about yourself as a TD professional? What soft skills do you require to be effective and successful in your career? Have you ever thought about all the skills in which you need to be proficient?

ATD's Talent Development Capability Model helps you define what technical skills you need to improve, but you need to look beyond the short capability statements to understand the soft skills required to support each (you can find the complete model on page 40). Let's examine a few examples where soft skills are required in each of the domains.

- **Building Personal Capability** is dedicated to soft skills, although all soft skills may not be called out. It's clear that communication, emotional intelligence, decision making, collaboration, cultural awareness, ethical behavior, and lifelong learning are soft skills.

Project management may be more technical, but you can't have a successful project without great communication and teamwork.

- **Developing Professional Capability** requires soft skills throughout. Could instructional design, delivery, and facilitation exist without creativity? You can't coach or attend to career development without paying attention to emotional intelligence (EI) and influence. Even technology application and knowledge management require TD professionals to be adaptable, creative, and team players for success.

- **Impacting Organizational Capability** focuses on the soft skills you'll use while working at the leadership and organizational level. For you to have business insight, be a partner with management, and develop organizational culture, you will need to build teamwork with the C-suite, practice influencing, and use your EI skills to communicate with them. Working on a talent strategy will require adaptability and influence. And you can't have successful change without excellent communication, EI, and teamwork. Future readiness is going to require creativity and innovation.

Simply put, soft skills are the attributes that enable TD professionals to interact effectively with others to achieve the 23 capabilities that span the spectrum of disciplines in the Capability Model.

Soft Skills: The Key to Professionalism

So, as TD professionals we need to be proficient in almost all soft skills to fulfill the most basic responsibilities of the job. However, there's something even more foundational to the importance of developing our soft skills: Only once we've mastered these skills can we project the professionalism that will garner respect from our stakeholders, our learners, and our peers. We must be professional, or why else are we called TD professionals?

Professionalism is the driving force to advance our careers. To earn the title of TD professional we need to be high performers and exhibit the qualities and skills that go beyond the list of technical TD skills. We need to be soft-skill proficient to deliver services with aplomb. We need to be team members to demonstrate we work well with others. We need to be EI-fluent to ensure that we are aware of, control, and express our emotions and handle interpersonal relationships well. We need to be creative to help our organization achieve a competitive advantage. We need to be adaptable to future-proof our organizations. And we need influencing skills that help us earn that proverbial seat at the table.

We all need role-specific knowledge and skills to perform our jobs, but those who achieve the most are also proficient in soft skills. You will use these skills every day of your life, in just about every interaction you have with others. Soft skills allow you to demonstrate flexibility, resourcefulness, and resilience—and as a result, enhance your professionalism and ensure career success. And a lack of them may just limit your career potential.

Clearly, soft skills are more critical than once thought and for TD professionals and trainers they are likely to be even more critical. Your participants and customers expect you to be on the leading edge of most topics that you deliver. And they also expect you to model the skills required for a successful career. So, which soft skills do you need to become a *professional* TD professional? Is it clearer communication? Interpersonal savvy? Increased flexibility? Self-management? Professional presence? Resourcefulness?

E.E. Cummings said, "It takes courage to grow up and become who you really are." I hope that you have the courage to determine which skills you need to improve to be the best trainer you can be—and especially to identify those misnamed soft skills that aren't soft at all. Then establish standards for yourself that are high enough to keep you on your training toes. The five books in the ATD Soft Skills Series offer you a great place to start.

Elaine Biech, Author
Skills for Career Success: Maximizing Your Potential at Work

Introduction

On March 16, 2020, I just happened to be working remotely. I took my car to the dealership for servicing that day. While I was working on my laptop in the customer waiting lounge, Michigan Gov. Gretchen Whitmer appeared on television to issue an order for the statewide closure of all restaurants and bars due to the spread of the coronavirus. Just three days prior, Michigan had banned gatherings of 250 or more. Then, less than 30 days later, business closures expanded to include nonessential workplaces.

During the course of the week, my thoughts were on my family and their well-being. I wondered if any of my family members had been exposed. I could not help but ponder what they were not telling us, since the situation had escalated to the serious level that required us to stay home for a stated period of time. My secondary focus was on what I'd needed to do to comply with the safety practices recommended by the Centers for Disease Control and Prevention and other experts. Initially, it was all surreal; I thought that this was something we'd only see in the movies. But no, this was our new reality, and I knew it was no time to panic. There were too many lingering questions. I wanted to know how long this would last and how the way I worked would have to change.

What began as remote work for one day that week turned into working remotely until further notice; stay-at-home orders likewise spread across the country. I had no idea that this was only the beginning of a new normal, to which I and everyone else would need to adapt. I recall thinking back to our last staff meeting in the office, which had happened less than two weeks prior to the lockdown. We were told the number of work-at-home days we would have for the year, and I thought

I might need to request more. Now that we were under the mandate of the lockdown, more would be allotted to every employee. I welcomed the luxury of working from home, but not for the reasons we had to do it. Potential time saved without a necessary commute to work and other business obligations appealed to me. Yet I felt anxious about getting more information from my organization on work expectations. Close friends had been working from home for more than 10 years and often shared what they appreciated about it. Not everyone is suited for working from home, but I believed that I was, and I was ready to put myself to the test.

What a shock the pandemic created for business, education, entertainment, travel, government, community, and daily life. In March, no one knew what to expect. No one knew what changes we would face as a result. We were about to find out what adaptability would demand of us. Our experience with COVID-19 is the perfect example of the importance of adaptability as a foundational skill, particularly at work. But the pandemic did not initiate the need for adaptability in the workplace. How many times before had you faced unanticipated changes requiring you to adjust?

Adaptability Is the New Game Changer

What does adaptability mean to you? What are its characteristics? What visuals come to mind? For me, I imagine a chameleon that's camouflaged perfectly with a tree branch in the midst of a rain forest. While we might strive to emulate the chameleon, it's not easy.

Adaptability means our ability to respond to unanticipated changes or new conditions in our environment. It also means our ability to not just face those changes, but also overcome adversity or modify ourselves for a new purpose. Those who rise to the challenge with the resilience, flexibility, and versatility demanded of them can always be distinguished from others. These individuals answer the call for transformation that challenges them to do the very thing that others say can't be done. Is that you?

In this book, you'll learn more about yourself, as well as why adaptability must be a part of who you are in order to achieve success.

Unanticipated changes provoke emotional reactions in us that influence our ability to adapt. This is one reason adaptability is strongly connected to emotional intelligence and recognized as an essential skill in work behavior. Emotional intelligence (also called emotional quotient, or EQ) is the ability to perceive, assess, and manage both your own and others' emotions. Individuals with a high EQ have a greater ability to adapt to change. Daniel Goleman is known for introducing how we can account for a person's emotional intelligence. Goleman's EQ Model covers four quadrants: self-awareness, social awareness, relationship management, and self-management:

- **Self-awareness** addresses the ability to recognize and understand your own emotions.
- **Social awareness** addresses the ability to understand the emotions, needs, and concerns of other people, as well as the ability to pick up on emotional cues and feel comfortable socially.
- **Relationship management** addresses awareness of your own emotions and those of others to build strong relationships. It includes the identification, analysis, and management of relationships with people inside and outside your team, as well as their development through feedback and coaching.
- **Self-management** is the discipline and management of one's internal states, impulses, and resources. It includes resilience, stress management, personal agility, and adapting to change.

In particular, self-management is where adaptability comes into play through the awareness and discipline to control and positively direct one's feelings. How well we handle our emotions when a challenge arises speaks to our ability to adapt. We manage our feelings, thoughts, and actions in flexible ways to get the desired results. Out of self-management, we arrive at the adaptability quotient, AQ, as a completely separate level of intelligence. AQ is the measure of one's ability to adapt.

I have firsthand experience with adaptability personally and professionally. Having held lead roles for managing change efforts in organizations, I have observed the benefits of adaptability at the individual and management levels. As I learned more about AQ in relation to the change management models and theories I had studied and applied at work, I became more captivated by this adaptability quotient. AQ is clearly rising in importance. Further research showed that AQ was not just another "Q" for thought, which we'll discuss in more detail over the course of the book.

Our Brain and Adaptability

We have to get our head in the game when change comes our way—expected or not. We can learn so much by understanding what happens with the brain when we are presented with unanticipated changes or new conditions. When a threat is reduced, it influences our adaptability level while boosting resilience and capability. This explains why individuals approach work and respond to workplace situations in a certain way. Ongoing research into neuroscience continues to reveal more about how the human brain works and its effect on adaptability.

Our brain is at the center of everything we do. The brain learns to hardwire repeated behaviors, which makes it resistant to change. Understanding aspects of neuroscience can inform us about adaptability. We know that change is inevitable. However, what happens with our brains when we respond to change is not something we may know. Our brain shifts into protective mode when it encounters change, responding to the stress of the situation. When we experience situations that are difficult or threatening, we feel the mental and physical state of stress. Brain functionality during this time can often dictate our response to changes thrust upon us.

What key brain parts are activated when we face new conditions, unexpected change, or a crisis? Three regions of the brain are involved with our perception and response to threats and stressors. They are the prefrontal cortex, amygdala, and hippocampus.

- **The prefrontal cortex** is home to our executive functioning, and regulates thoughts and emotions. It allows us to do analytical problem solving, abstract thinking, planning, and future forecasting.
- **The amygdala** oversees our emotional responses, such as anxiety, fear, and aggression. It turns on stress hormones and increases the heart rate. The prefrontal cortex helps maintain control and works with the amygdala in how we view stressful events.
- **The hippocampus** is the memory center of the brain. It forms and stores memories and functions as our central area for learning. We retrieve memories from related experiences and store memories for new experiences when the hippocampus is triggered.

Our memories stay with us; they're based on what we have learned and what we have experienced emotionally. Think about the special events you remember, such as your wedding, the birth of a child, the death of a loved one, a scary amusement park ride, your first job, your best vacation, your college graduation, or your first promotion. Once a person encounters a stressful situation, it can be easy to revert to past behavior if you recall a similar experience you had. Those who cower under pressure or become emotionally unstable in response to change may have developed this pattern of behavior in response to events in their past. Others who are able to face a crisis or new conditions with an openness to gaining information, considering options, and calmly making a decision may have developed this pattern of doing so instead. We have the ability to train our brains to adapt.

Consider what steps you can take with this knowledge to improve your adaptability. Recognizing your triggers and emotional behaviors in certain instances can assist you with recognizing areas where greater control is needed. Say that you become frustrated when you are challenged. Once you recognize this, you can work on managing yourself by adjusting your perception of another viewpoint, asking clarifying questions to hear opposing viewpoints, or removing yourself from the situation temporarily to allow yourself time to think. When this is done successfully, we can view it as an increase in adaptability.

How This Book Will Help You

As we become more informed about adaptability, opportunities to exercise adaptability become apparent. Maybe you have not considered it or even realized that your ability to adapt is a big deal. Why, you may ask? Change is constant. Change is inevitable. Change is a part of progress. But responding to change requires skill, along with a certain level of capability and training. More discussion on these will explain how they are distinguished.

Talent development professionals face countless situations that can reveal how much of a tolerance one has for unanticipated change. Relentless change in technology keeps the modalities of learning dynamic. As organizations become more agile and responsive to change, talent development professionals can position themselves strategically to assist in the alignment of training and business goals. The endless search for a competitive advantage places great demands on organizations to build strong learning cultures that cater to current and future job roles. Organizations have instructor-led training (ILT), e-learning, and artificial intelligence, but need guidance in moving strategically from pushing these training options to enabling employees to pull what they need on demand. My work with a few clients has been geared to promoting their learning strategy and how they want to brand it internally before promoting it outside the organization. Clients have shared with me their struggles in creating more experiential leadership development. I have worked with others to design learning for working remotely and prove the value of training to stakeholders. To keep a finger on the pulse of L&D and client needs, I have maintained a mindset that has been open to evolving my role.

When I left the public sector and entered into the private sector, I needed to adapt. I had been working for a city government in Michigan for 20 years, within a few city departments. One of the biggest adjustments for me was moving from a predominantly African American workforce with thousands of workers to being the only African American worker in an organization of around 20. Although I went into the situation with knowledge of the culture and race differences, I still faced other unanticipated changes and new circumstances that required me to adapt in some ways I did not foresee: the types of customer needs, resources to meet those needs, my approach to consulting on those needs, and a workforce that received a heavy dose of diversity from me joining their all-white organization. We had clients outside the US, which meant being conscious of things I had previously taken for granted while servicing those within the city and those involved in ATD chapter projects. Some client and project needs warranted vendor partnering or seeking a resource in our freelance network when we did not have one internally. I adjusted from being the only resource for my talent development projects to being one of multiple resources for completing a project. I had to adapt to working solely on what was applicable to my role, consulting with the client, and sometimes leading the other third-party resources in completing work on the project. In this experience, I also realized how intertwined diversity, equity, and inclusion (DEI) were with adaptability.

Our adaptability is tested by how we interact with team members, what tools we use to get the work done, and how we respond to ever-changing training needs of a diverse target audience. Think back to your last experience facing unplanned change in the type of training you designed, the way you facilitated training, the selection or implementation of a learning management system (LMS), the way you handled a learning project, or how you consulted with stakeholders in the C-suite on your organization's learning needs. Your skill in adaptability can serve you in whatever role you have, as well as in your leadership capability, career potential, and working relationships. Take note of areas and ways you can better adapt on an individual level as you read this book.

Workplace changes are leading the need to reinvent learning and development for a future-ready workforce with enhanced technology integration. For example, virtual training is now a norm for many organizations, whether they were prepared before the pandemic or not. Recently, one of my clients had me train their staff on best practices in conducting virtual instructor-led training (VILT) because they needed to adapt and switch the launch of their internal leadership curriculum from in-person to online. Companies around the world found themselves in the same predicament—workplace learning had to continue, but had to adapt to the circumstances.

And adaptability holds importance for survival, profitability, and competitiveness, as businesses embark on digitization and transformation. We've seen businesses suffer or close because their operation required or allowed for large groups of people to be in proximity, with direct contact. Some businesses are still recovering, and many are adapting and moving forward with new ways of doing business.

In 2020, I was the past president of ATD Detroit, a local chapter of the Association for Talent Development. Similar to other talent development organizations, we looked at alternative ways to hold events, partner with other organizations, and promote our value proposition while delivering quality services and benefits for our customers. We adapted by teaming up with numerous ATD chapters to increase our reach, reduce expenses, and enhance our service offerings. We also took creative and innovative steps with virtual events. We provided increased special interest groups, lunch chats, and additional resource services to members. Like many organizations, we realized the growth that is possible when the business demonstrates adaptability in response to adverse situations.

Ready to Adapt?

Your journey to developing adaptability will lead you through a growth process that can propel you personally and professionally. We'll start with a deeper exploration into why adaptability is the new game changer in talent development. You'll follow the story of a small business owner who faced ruin, but rather than give up, turned it around. And you'll read about a surfer who had to overcome extreme circumstances and adapt against the odds.

The second part of the book will take you on a thrill ride to learn how and where to put adaptability into practice as a talent development professional whom any organization would value on their team. The close of each chapter will direct you to do some reflection. As you reflect, ask yourself if there is something that resonates with you, what you have learned that can enhance your capability, and where you see opportunity for your own development.

Over the course of the book, you'll encounter various tools and resources, such as the Talent Development Capability Model, an AQ Model, the ADAPT Model, a Cheat Sheet for Adaptability, and the Career Adaptability Checklist. Use the models and tools to reinforce the content, build your confidence, and demonstrate your adaptability in any role you may hold in talent development. Employ the checklists to break down the application steps in certain areas.

Always see potential by looking beyond what's normal in your life, because change is inevitable. Use the knowledge, resources, and tools in this book to guide you in developing an attitude of adaptability that you will put into action. Look for ways to apply the tools to your work and career journey. Some sections will walk you through reflective steps for increased self-awareness that will be valuable to your development and growth. Adaptability is one skill that we may label differently in the future. For example, in the past the push was to build leaders with people skills, which today has the more appropriate label of emotional intelligence. Regardless of what we call it, the need for adaptability will never go away.

PART 1
The Case for Adaptability

CHAPTER 1

The Subtle Art of Adaptability

A carpenter's passion was the building block of the successful woodworking shop he founded in 1916, producing furniture such as ladders, stools, and ironing boards. Almost 10 years later, his sons started an accidental fire that caused all his dreams and his home to go up in flames. Instead of quitting, he decided to build a larger workshop. Almost 10 years after that, his wife passed away. During this time, he also encountered financial hardship with the business. Because of the loss he experienced, the woodshop owner decided to create inexpensive products such as cheap toys, which led him into bankruptcy. Refusing to give up his passion, he continued with his company and renamed it to reflect its new direction. The new name was taken from *leg godt*, which was Latin for "play well." The company became known as LEGO, and Ole Kirk Christiansen, the woodshop owner, persevered with adaptability to become an industry giant.

What Does Adaptability Mean?

Adaptability, and its appearance in humans and all other species, has been a topic of discussion for millennia. In fact, Aristotle and Empedocles were two Greek philosophers who introduced us to adaptation. Aristotle posited that an organism's features and characteristics are a result of environmental influences. These influences inform our understanding of adaptability.

As we get into the subtle art of adaptability, let's revisit what adaptability is—the ability to respond to unanticipated changes or new conditions in our environment. Often, *flexibility* and *versatility* are also thrown around as synonyms. However, for the context of this book, I have come to view them slightly differently. At a basic level, *flexibility* is having the ability to change or be changed easily based on the situation. *Versatility* means having a variety of abilities. I also like the distinction that Tony Alessandra and Michael J. O'Connor make between flexibility and versatility in their book *The Platinum Rule* (1998): They explain flexibility as your attitude or willingness to adapt, while versatility is your ability to adapt.

Based on Alessandra and O'Connor's explanation of flexibility and versatility as two components of adaptability, we can gain greater appreciation for adaptability at work personally and professionally. These components not only contribute to our description of adaptability, but also give us a view of it as something within our power to control. Of course, we know that unanticipated changes cannot be controlled. That leaves our response to those unanticipated changes as the thing within our control.

When I was laid off almost 10 years ago, I encountered a situation for some self-discovery with my flexibility and versatility. During my time with the city government, I received multiple promotions working in the training division for our HR department. We conducted training for more than 14,000 city employees. Then, because of budget cuts, they dissolved the training division. After nearly 15 years, this came as a shock, although I should have seen it coming. They offered me a demotion with a $30,000 pay cut, which would allow me to keep my benefits and remain on the payroll in a permanent position. I declined and decided to focus on increasing my marketability and putting my job search into overdrive. One week after I declined the demotion, they offered me a contractual role at my previous salary, but with no benefits. I thought it over, prayed about it, and decided to accept this contractual role as an instructional designer for the human resource information system (HRIS) implementation project in the IT department.

In the new role, I used more blended learning approaches and more advanced technology, worked with a multicultural staff at a different location, and focused more on technical training. I viewed this as an opportunity to rise to the challenge, because it was completely outside my area of expertise and comfort zone. I had the versatility. I knew that I could learn whatever I put my mind to, and I was acutely aware of my potential at the time. I did not view this change as the opportunity it eventually turned out to be for my career. Yet, on reflection, it became a testament to my adaptability, flexibility, and versatility. Your adaptability journey will require looking to your past experiences and reactions, because they will inform how you're able to adapt in the future.

It's a Matter of Perception and Perspective

Perception and perspective are two driving factors for adaptability. Perception is the mental grasp you have of something through the use of your senses, while your perspective is your point of view. I held the belief that the lens through which I was viewing the world ultimately shaped my interpretation of that view. However, that is not the case. It is actually your perception that dictates your perspective.

In *The Seven Habits of Effective People*, Stephen R. Covey tells a poignant story that captures perception and perspective. Two battleships are at sea and are experiencing severe weather. A signalman reports to the captain that he sees a light. When the captain inquires, the signalman informs the captain that another ship appears to be on a collision course with them. The captain instructs the signalman to advise the other ship to change course by 20 degrees. The other ship signals back with the same, advising to change course by 20 degrees. The captain tells the signalman, "Send, 'I'm a captain; change course 20 degrees.'" They receive a reply, "I'm a seaman second class, who advises that they change course 20 degrees." In an outrage, the captain instructs the signalman to send the message that they are a battleship, so the other ship should change course. The seaman responds with a flashing light: "I'm a lighthouse." The captain realized his ship had to change course. Covey shares the story to explain the importance of being open to a paradigm shift. His idea of a paradigm shift requires the willingness to re-evaluate one's perception and adjust your perspective as needed.

My initial experience with ATD created a vivid personal picture of perception and perspective. When I was in the city government position, my manager, Mr. Bridges, encouraged me to join our local ATD chapter. This was just a short time after I'd earned a master's degree in instructional technology. He explained that this would be a great move for my career, my network, and my exposure to what is current in training and development. I took his advice, as I usually did, and decided to attend a chapter meeting. Based on this experience, I joined the chapter, only to find out that my job was discontinuing reimbursements for professional memberships because of budget cuts. That did it for me. I wasn't completely sold on the idea of this added expense, considering my salary at the time.

Some years later, my perception changed when I experienced the layoff mentioned previously. I went from viewing a potential ATD Detroit chapter membership as an expense to viewing it as an essential investment in enhancing my marketability. Instead of walking away, I ran to ATD Detroit with a new perception that affected my perspective. How was I able to do this? It was due to my perception of the situation. The reality I was seeing dictated my point of view.

Reflect on situations you have encountered in your life where your perspective was not too favorable because your perception was negative. Now think about how your perspective might have been different if you'd been able to improve your perception—your adaptability.

🔅 Consider This

- How do I define adaptability?
- Where can I see evidence of my ability to adapt?

How We Respond to Uncertainty and Adversity

In his book *No Limits*, John Maxwell (2017) states, "The greatest separator between successful and unsuccessful people is how they deal with and explain their failures, problems, and difficulties." There is usually a story we tell ourselves regarding what we are experiencing amid adversity or unanticipated changes. Ole Kirk Christiansen could have told himself that his woodworking business was over or that it wasn't meant to be. But no. The story he told himself was one that had to inspire and drive him to keep going when situations were uncertain and obstacles were frequent. Regardless of how well the story is told, the question centers on what kind of story you are telling yourself. Amid change, we learn about who we are.

Changes create challenges or disruptions that require us to respond. Change is inevitable and it can happen in a variety of ways. At work, it could be a job change, process change, new team member, company merger, new product line, or business closure. In our personal lives, it could be having a child, starting college, getting lost, dealing with a car accident, or losing a loved one. How we respond is usually the result of our past experiences, education, and emotional state.

Adaptability often comes down to how we deal with times of uncertainty. Situations that make us feel unsure of a predictable future and as though we have no control leave us uncomfortable. They might even feel dangerous to us. Dealing with the unknown, or the lack of a clear picture of what is going to happen, forces us to rely on past experience or let our imagination have its way. In these instances, our mental strength is challenged. People may resort to trying to capture some aspect of control over events or other people, or they may revert to shutting down. Letting go is also a type of response. This could be letting go of:

- The need for things to go a certain way
- The idea that things should go as you imagine
- Things you don't actually control

- People who are not good for you
- A job that no longer makes you happy
- A negative story you may be telling yourself

Think about a time when the root of your problem was refusing to let go of the idea that you have to get everything right or be right all the time. This worked in my favor when I was rejected a second time for a proposal that I believed was very well written and met more than the requirements. I let go of the thought that I would never get the approval or proposals would continue to be rejected because I didn't have what it took. Letting go is a positive course of action, unlike shutting down, which happens when uncertainty causes us to feel overwhelmed. To avoid the worry, frustration, stress, and other feelings that can overwhelm us, we can identify how adaptability skills benefit us in uncertain times.

We can learn more about our individual ability to adapt by closely examining common negative and positive responses when we face adversity or a change. Negative responses or thoughts might include:

- "I knew something would go wrong."
- "I'm just not cut out for this."
- "That's too much to handle."
- "I don't see how we can make this work."
- "It sounded too good to be true."
- "Well, someone else needs to figure out a way out of this."

How many times do you recall yourself stating or thinking along these lines when you were dealing with a situation that seemed like it was too much for you to handle? This is not to say that if you've ever had these thoughts, you're lacking in adaptability. But if you have a pattern of this line of responding or thinking, it's worth exploring. These responses can be observed in behavior—it might be stressing out, getting frustrated, shutting down, or being pessimistic. Booker T. Washington said, "I have begun everything with the idea that I could succeed, and I never had much patience with the multitudes of people who are always ready to explain why one cannot succeed." Usually, it is easy for us to recognize patterns of negativity in others. It takes intentionality to reflect on our own behavior to see if there is opportunity for improvement in this area.

On the flip side, positive types of responses that are characteristic of individuals with high adaptability skills include:

- "Things will work out. Let's rethink this."
- "I was built for this."
- "I can figure out a way to handle this."
- "We can do this. There must be a way to make this work."
- "I think this is an opportunity to try something different."
- "Give me some time to think this through and come up with another option."

Are these your default responses to adversity? As I mentioned, we are talking about a pattern of behavior or line of thinking indicative of someone with high adaptability skills. Such behaviors can include thinking out of the box, stepping out of your comfort zone, being willing to learn something new, or quickly adjusting when transitioning among multiple tasks.

Here's a situation where I was forced to turn the magnifying glass on my own behavior. I was working on contract with the city for a special project for an HRIS implementation. I was one instructional designer on a team of three, and I enjoyed the role despite the extreme change from my previous role in HR. The project reached a point where a new system was selected for the implementation, and an external consulting company was coming in to manage it for the whole city. Our team was asked to gather all source documents, files, spreadsheets, and custom work we created so they could be provided to the external team, which would take over what we were doing. That was a major change, and I told myself once again that I had stayed with the city too long.

We had our watercooler talks and the feeling was mutual on our team that it was a problem to just package everything nicely for others to walk in and take over. Of course, it felt worse for me, because I was the only one on our team who had been laid off and was working on contract. At first, I could not bring myself to get on board with this change. But then I realized I had to re-evaluate and reflect on what I was thinking and saying. These things were not happening to me. I had decided to stay with the city and not aggressively pursue other opportunities, because I was working on my doctorate at the time. I accepted the contractual role. I chose what I was going to make happen rather than things happening to me. How often do we fail to acknowledge this?

I ended up taking the lead on gathering everything for handoff. I did it because I believed that regardless of whom it was helping, I had to stick to my principles. I applied empathy along with adaptability because I also thought about how I would feel if I were the vendor coming into the situation. Did I really want to sabotage the project by sitting out? I created a spreadsheet and organized the information, files, links, and much more by category and file type.

What happened next, I honestly did not expect. When I submitted everything to our manager, she asked to see me in her office. I knew I had done a thorough job with the organization and inclusion of necessary resources, so I figured she was going to thank me and give me a date for my contract termination. Surprisingly, she asked me if I was interested in taking the role of change management training lead on the city side to work with the other companies involved. Here was a leadership opportunity to build my skills in an area where I had almost no experience. This story hits at the heart of the importance of self-reflection, with special attention given to our pattern of thinking.

The Adaptability Quotient

So if change is inevitable and varied, where do flexibility, versatility, perspective, and perception lead us on our adaptability journey? We arrive at the adaptability quotient (AQ) as a tool to measure those things and recognize their importance. AQ was originally introduced by Paul Stoltz in 1997. He introduced it as the adversity quotient, but it has come to be used interchangeably with the adaptability quotient. Similar to IQ and EQ, AQ gauges one's adaptability skills. Think of your AQ as your adaptability score; this book will help you aim high.

Not until recent years have we come to see that adaptability's reach extends beyond the challenges of keeping up with technological change at breakneck speeds. Business and workplace changes, the consequences of COVID-19, and L&D changes have left us in severe states of uncertainty and adverse situations. This has prompted the need for businesses that can thrive in these states. For this to happen, leaders and workers at various levels in an organization must have the adaptability skills to not only survive, but thrive.

EQ skills gained the spotlight when we recognized how important it is to appreciate and respect the human element in work interactions, especially given the increasing use of technology. Now we see prevalence of adaptability skills. What good is my ability to deal with people and myself in different situations if I cannot keep pace and adjust as changes arise that are outside my control? Natalie Fratto explains it: "Adaptability is not just the capacity to absorb new information, but the ability to work out what is relevant, to unlearn obsolete knowledge, to overcome challenges, and to make a conscious effort to change" (Murray 2019). AQ is taking its place alongside EQ.

Adaptability Skills and Traits

To learn how we can improve our adaptability, let's break down adaptability into two buckets: skills and traits. We are born with traits, also known as natural talents, whereas skills are abilities we learn. We develop some adaptability skills as a result of our education, professional development, coaching, and mentoring. Of course, some examples may fall in both areas, such as creativity and flexibility. For example, I have a nephew who has been creative since I started observing him closely at the age of two, so this is a trait of his. I had to learn and develop my creative skills.

What are some of those adaptability skills? Skills in high-AQ individuals include:

- **Curiosity:** strong desire to know or learn something
- **Effective communication:** successful exchange of ideas, thoughts, knowledge, and information via speaking, writing, or another medium
- **Innovation:** introduction or implementation of a new or improved product, process, or service
- **Learning agility:** ability to learn and unlearn from experience and then apply new learning to new situations
- **Motivation:** ability to stimulate interest or willingness to do something
- **Negotiation:** discussion aimed at resolving an issue or reaching an agreement
- **Problem solving:** finding the solution to a problem
- **Resilience:** ability to adapt to change and recover quickly or bounce back
- **Strategic thinking:** analyzing problems from a broad perspective to come up with viable strategies in line with an organization's objectives

> **Consider This**
> - What adaptability skills and traits do I demonstrate?
> - Where do I have opportunity to improve my adaptability skills?

Adaptability skills are common, and you may not always recognize them as being connected to adaptability. Sure, we all have moments when we tell ourselves something like, "Innovative, motivating, resilient, and versatile; oh yeah, that's me!" Yet these skills are sometimes missing when you are in the middle of a crisis, or when a new circumstance requires you to rise to the occasion. There are a few reasons for that. One is that certain skills may appear to be natural tendencies, even though you learned them. Another reason is that we may not have clarity on what adaptability truly is. Finally, many of us have not viewed adaptability as being important enough to have specific skills associated with it—until now.

While skills are learned, traits make us who we are. Traits of adaptability should not be foreign to you. In fact, you may have seen them at work within yourself or others, so let's cover some examples:

- **Creative:** ability to use one's imagination to create something new
- **Enterprising:** one who organizes the business venture and assumes the risk for it
- **Flexible:** ability to change or be changed easily
- **Optimistic:** one who is inclined to be hopeful and expects a favorable outcome
- **Positive:** quality of being encouraging or promising of a successful outcome
- **Resourceful:** ability to cope with difficulties
- **Risk taker:** someone who takes a chance with potential loss or injury in the hope of gain or excitement
- **Self-starter:** a person who begins work or undertakes a project on their own initiative
- **Versatile:** having a variety of abilities

Because traits are a part of us with or without building skills, we need to take them into consideration as we look at how we work toward developing our adaptability skills.

Paul Stoltz went as far as to recognize categories of adaptability skills based on people's pursuit of purpose in life and work. Stoltz references this pursuit as their ascent up a mountain. He identifies the categories as quitters, campers, and climbers:

- **Quitters** are those who abandoned their pursuit of purpose in the midst of a challenge and gave up on reaching their potential.

- **Campers** are those who reached half of their potential because they stopped their pursuit after getting to a certain point. They no longer rise to the challenge when they face adversity.
- **Climbers** are those who consistently rise to the challenge that others flee in fear. Climbers do not accept defeat and are able to use their challenges to learn, adapt, and grow as they proceed to their next mountain.

Many of us can easily recognize climbers as the group that would reflect many adaptability skills and traits. Campers and quitters help us to understand those who once exhibited these skills, but no longer exhibit that drive. These categories are useful in understanding what is demanded of adaptable workers with adaptability skills. We will revisit these categories in part 2, "Putting Adaptability Into Practice."

Your AQ Moments

Unanticipated change can put a high-AQ person's creativity and innovation into high gear. In contrast, a low-AQ person may shift to hopelessness, fear, and frustration. When you recognize which one you are, you can then set goals for improvement based on your status. I encourage you to consider the adaptability behaviors you exhibit in various professional and personal situations. Reflect on your flexibility and versatility in those instances. Ask yourself if you need to change your perception as a way of influencing your perspective, which could result in you demonstrating better flexibility and versatility. Your adaptability skills in action will always begin and end with you. I encourage you to pursue new heights as you work to be the mountain climber you were meant to be, because AQ is the new game changer.

CHAPTER 2

Survival of the Fittest: Why Adaptability Matters

Management studies author and professor Leon C. Megginson (1963) said, "It is not the strongest or the most intelligent who will survive, but those who can best manage change." This business adage resembles Charles Darwin's theory of natural selection, which posits that animals' instincts aid their survival, and builds on Aristotle's theory of environmental fit mentioned in the previous chapter. I believe we are all fit to survive, and adaptability is one of the keys to survival in life and at work. That is why adaptability matters.

How do you face adversity when your life depends on it? Can we apply this to adaptability in your work role? You can be the judge when we look at the life of a remarkable woman. Araminta "Minty" Ross worked as a cook and a nurse in the US military. Few know that she was also the first woman to lead an armed expedition during wartime after growing up in slavery. Growing up, she watched as her family was sent to different plantations and received a head injury that left an affliction she would endure for the rest of her life. This singular person was no other than Harriet Tubman, whom we also know as "Moses"—the one who helped free more than 700 slaves via the Underground Railroad. After experiences with severe mistreatment of slaves, she decided that she had to initiate a change in response to the adversity she faced. She modeled leadership with a vision, decision making in figuring out ways of escape, innovative thinking in pursuit of freedom, and resilience amid her struggles. For many of us, our struggles are not nearly as severe. However, her story depicts the adaptability you put to work in response to unanticipated change.

Today, we fight not against slavery but for DEI, in order to embrace cultural change in organizations. While our response to the COVID-19 pandemic might be freshest in your mind, we see the power and potential of human adaptability in every facet of our lives. Organizational changes resulting in job cuts have forced many to seek alternative sources of income. Change is not confined to the workplace; we see it in the world around us, too. Skills in adapting to world changes make the difference in our ability to cope with change on the job.

Why Adaptability Matters to You

Our ability to adjust to business climate changes reflects what we experience in our brain. These are the changes happening in the three regions of the brain that were explained in the introduction. Let's say you learn that a scheduled technical training course needs to be revised because of a change in the system employees are being trained to use. While you are thinking about how much work is involved, if it is too much to handle, if it is just a minor change, or if this is something to be expected, your brain is responding as a result. This is commonly known as the "fight or flight" response. You are choosing to deal with the change because you think you can handle it—fight. The response when you feel as if you're in over your head is flight. They are both mental modes of responding that reflect brain plasticity. You see yourself as either built for the job or not cut out for the job. This is the reason some people become stressed, fearful, angry, or overwhelmed, which can manifest as depression, heart issues, or other illnesses. For others, the response may be ambivalence, enthusiasm, and optimism, which may have some positive bodily benefits. According to the American Institute of Stress, 83 percent of US workers experience job-related stress, and more than 75 percent of health conditions can be attributed to stress (Milenkovic 2019). Your perception of change and your ability to handle it determine the physiological effects you experience.

At the behavioral level, the ways we adapt are much more apparent. Behaviors tend to reflect our thought processes. Behaviors that represent adaptability lead us to face a new situation head-on: collaborating with others, asking questions, sharing creative and innovative ideas, motivating team members, and demonstrating a willingness to take risks. Behaviors that represent poor adaptability include complaining, blaming others, making excuses, increased absenteeism, staying in a comfort zone, and focusing on old or traditional ways. The power of the mind makes it a key factor in our ability to not only adapt but also exhibit high behavioral adaptability.

Charles Duhigg explains how our behaviors develop into habits, and how we can develop new habits. Once a behavior becomes automatic, it is a habit. Duhigg (2012) states that 40 percent of our daily behaviors are based on habits with minimal, if any, decision making involved, because the brain does not have to be fully engaged when we are acting automatically. The benefit is that habits save our brain energy, because we have developed a routine, such as taking a shower each morning, getting a daily coffee, commuting to work, answering the phone, checking email, and driving. We can evaluate our habits to determine where there is opportunity for AQ development. When you face a dilemma that comes out of the blue at work or there is a change in direction from leadership, how do you typically respond? Do you feel that your behavior in those instances reflects that of an adaptable person? You will discover how to change habits in order to reflect high AQ in part 2.

We can change our willingness and ability to adapt, and we can learn about others who are great models of success. A number of individuals have modeled examples of adaptability. I must admit that I place Barack Obama near the top of the list. It required such a high level of adaptability to become president of the United States. In an interview, Obama talked about adapting to a life with no blueprint or precedent as the first African American to hold the highest office in the nation.

Malala Yousafzai gives us an example with her life, which she nearly lost as she fought to receive an education in Pakistan despite threats from the Taliban. She survived a gunshot wound to the head in 2012, when she was 15. Her drive to fight for women's right to education distinguished her. "I raise up my voice—not so I can shout, but so that those without a voice can be heard," she said in a 2013 address to the United Nations Youth Assembly. "We cannot succeed when half of us are held back." Her innovative thinking, optimism, and other works of activism led to her being the youngest person to receive the Nobel Peace Prize in 2014.

Some of the amenities we use in our daily lives are the result of individuals showing us the power of adaptability and innovation. Richard Spikes did just that with his 1932 invention of the automatic gearshift in cars. His innovation changed our experience of driving with the ability to have all gears engaged and switch between them automatically as needed. Or consider your morning cup of coffee; you probably have Melitta Bentz of Germany to thank for it. In her search to address the problems of grainy coffee, over-brewing, and tiresome filter cleaning, she invented a coffee filter system in 1908.

Have you ever thought about what creation or invention might make your work or personal life easier? These individuals saw a need to be met, an idea to be improved, or a right to be upheld. Through their efforts, they are role models of adaptability. You too can deliver tangible benefits to clients and customers with adaptability skills.

☀️ Consider This

- Who are my models of adaptability?
- How would someone characterize my typical response to unanticipated change?

Why Adaptability Matters in the Workplace

We can look to the evidence that substantiates the importance of adaptability in the workplace:

- 91 percent of HR decision makers expect the ability to cope with change and uncertainty to be a skill in demand for new employees (Talent Economy).
- 67 percent of companies expect workers to adapt and pick up skills in the course of changing jobs (World Economic Forum 2018).
- 50 percent of today's jobs will not exist by 2030 (Ettling 2015).
- 42 percent of L&D professionals identify creative problem solving and design thinking as one of the top five skills in high demand (LinkedIn 2020).

This data gives us a glimpse of what is on the horizon for the workplace. By the year 2030, L&D positions will not look like they do today, and that also applies to jobs across the board. Workers face not only the accelerating pace of the advancing technology, but also the new ways of working that they must embrace. There is a skill to this, and it is called adaptability.

We cannot blame everything that has gone wrong on COVID-19. The pandemic magnified changes that were already apparent at the business level. *Forbes* reported business closings and bankruptcy filings for companies such as Advantage Rent a Car, Frontier Communications, GNC, J.C. Penney, J.Crew, Neiman Marcus, Skillsoft, Virgin Australia, Whiting Petroleum, and more. This was all while companies like Amazon reported record profits. I am sure that very few of us can say that we did not place or receive an Amazon order during the initial 180 days of COVID-19. Stay-at-home orders declared around the world resulted in minimal to no in-person shopping, reduced travel, and business closures. The decreasing demand crippled economies worldwide. Not all organizations were able to adapt to the speed and impact of the unanticipated changes brought by COVID-19. In previous years, we've seen the failed adaptability of organizations such as BlackBerry, Blockbuster, Kodak, Sears, Toys "R" Us, and Xerox.

Looking further back, much business disruption has resulted from rapid technology advancement. In 1990, more than 50 percent of the Fortune 500's top 20 companies were from the oil and gas and automotive industries. The same list in 2020 has more than 50 percent of the top 20 represented by health and e-commerce industries. The oil and gas industry represents 20 percent of the 2020 list. From the 1990 list, only three companies remain in the top 20 for 2020—Exxon Mobil (number 3), Ford (number 12), and GM (number 18). As you can see, our economy is tough, competitive, and volatile. Checking the market, taking customers' pulse, leveraging the latest and greatest technology, digitization, and optimizing the web are major checkpoints in business that feed adaptability. Looking internally without looking externally and globally is another way businesses fail to tap into an opportunity. The pandemic simply made a bad situation worse.

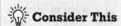 **Consider This**
- What are some observations that represent adaptability in my workplace?
- Why should I make adaptability a priority at the individual level?

Adaptability offers benefits beyond business survival. Benefits at the individual level include building a reputation of resilience and being a desirable job candidate. Take advantage of a situation where you have to pose a creative solution to a problem or share an idea that gives a competitive edge. For example, you may recommend a new approach for your team's hybrid collaboration to engage on-site and off-site workers. Your colleagues may look to you as someone who is always interested in learning more about those from a different culture and helping them feel included.

Consistently using your adaptability skills can position you as a key asset to your current or future organization. People recognize the strength of adaptability when they are able to see it as your habitual response. Moments that matter are those when your knee-jerk reactions are rooted to adaptability in a crisis or challenge. Reflect on times when you were able to come through for your team or organization in the heat of the moment. Maybe it was the moment your team decided to work from home during the pandemic, and something you did contributed to making things work. Or maybe it was a moment when your resiliency drove you to start doing L&D work as an independent contractor for additional income. What may have seemed like the worst of times was the cue for you to adapt, which catapulted you to the best of times.

A workplace benefits from a set culture. Workplaces demonstrating that they expect creativity, innovation, critical thinking, and so forth set the tone for workers to adapt and rise to the challenge. They are encouraged to model the behavior, which perpetuates a high level of adaptability throughout the organization. I envision an ideal workplace as one with these qualities, and I am sure you would as well.

Organizations with these types of cultures attract top talent. Branding is strengthened for the organization, which can help workers as well, because they're associated with the company. High-AQ individuals possess these qualities and they make up teams and leaders who are the key variables behind the success of a business. Reinforcement of a positive workplace image for workers and clients in this regard goes a long way. Companies such as Amazon, Apple, Facebook, Nike, and Tesla know this very well, because they rank in the top 20 for the most innovative and creative in a Visual Capitalist list (Ang 2020). This can promote employee engagement, growth, and retention. Extensive preparation is a good practice, but it does not overshadow the power of a business that is able to prove its strength in response to a crisis or unexpected challenges.

Adaptability Is Necessary

Still not convinced that adaptability is a need rather than a want? In matters of survival, we do what is necessary. This should be no different for business, your career, and certainly learning and development. Ongoing workplace disruption should keep us on a course of not simply surviving, but thriving with adaptability. If unexpected change always provokes you to flight or freeze, then your AQ is not as high as you may think. But the good news for all of us is this change is within your control. Adaptability may have made its debut early in human existence, but it has proved to be something we can implement to do more than just survive when it comes to one's career. Your work performance as an individual or on a team in high-pressure situations, a crisis, meetings, interviews, and negotiations can be maximized by your response to unplanned change.

CHAPTER 3

Against All Odds: Barriers to Adaptability

When it comes to adapting, persevering, and overcoming challenges, I always remember the plot of the movie *Soul Surfer*. For those not familiar, the movie is based on the life of Bethany Hamilton, a young surfer who resides in Kauai, Hawaii. During a surfing outing with friends, Bethany, age 13, is attacked by a shark and loses her whole left arm. As you can imagine, her recuperation is arduous, but her determination, perseverance, and passion for surfing lead her back to the water; she learns to surf with one arm. Staying on her board proved to be incredibly difficult with only one arm to help stabilize her. He father, showing his creativity and innovation, makes a special board that keeps her from sliding off. Eventually, Bethany decides to return to competing and places as one of the top performers in a local competition. In proving to herself and others that she is able to overcome her challenges, she demonstrates her adaptability.

Challenges and barriers have their place in our efforts to respond to the problems we don't see coming. Bethany's challenges were adapting to the loss of her arm, relearning her passion, and overcoming feeling different from the other competitors. There were barriers with her mental state in deciding to go back into the water, surfing with one arm, and not being able to stay on her surfboard. In this chapter, reflect on your challenges and barriers, and how you respond when it seems as if the odds are against you. Your challenges might not be as severe as losing your arm, but they feel just as real in the moment. As you reflect, my question for you is, are you willing to get back on the board?

Adaptability Misconceptions

Let's start with some common misconceptions about adaptability. For example, you might believe that adaptability is just a buzzword. In the last few years, it has grown in popularity in response to a breathtaking speed of disruption and change. This could be a reason behind its perception as a trend. Some undervalue adaptability and mistakenly view it as nonessential to job performance and career success. Contrary to what some may think, not everyone adapts successfully when it comes to work performance and career. That presents our reason for AQ, which measures our adaptability skills.

Or you might think that as long as you demonstrate a willingness to adapt, you don't have to worry about being able to adapt in real-life circumstances. This gets back to distinguishing between flexibility and versatility in the first chapter; being flexible and open to adapting is not the same as doing so. Related is the assumption that our biological instinct to adapt makes it automatic. Not true. There is no adaptability gene that will respond to all the changes our modern world can throw at us. It takes effort to put adaptability skills to work.

You might have the misconception that adaptability is needed only for a new workplace, a career change, a customer change or loss, or a business change. This narrow view limits the power that adaptability skills can have in all facets of your life. Imagine the challenge of starting a new business and facing the unexpected on a regular basis. What about deciding to relocate to another state for a new job or to be with family? How about choosing to pursue your graduate degree? The common denominator for these examples is the key determinant of success—adaptability.

Finally, there is the misconception that if your attempt to adapt fails, then it was a lost cause. This could not be further from the truth.

If nothing else, a failure moves us closer to the right answer and adds to our lessons learned. Hopefully by the end of this book, you won't be one of those individuals who stops at the first sign of failure.

So, by changing how you perceive what adaptability means, you can avoid allowing these false beliefs to be barriers to your adaptability and skill building for a high AQ.

Our Resilience Can Get in the Way

It might come as a surprise, but resilience itself can act as a potential barrier to adapting. That runs counter to the view that resilience is a good thing and appropriate in response to new circumstances. But let's give more thought to that.

Take a moment to reflect on what resilience means: the ability to bounce back. The problem is when resilience becomes an impediment to innovation and creativity due to a focus on returning to normal state. COVID-19 presented a prime example with our hope to return to a pre-pandemic normal. Yet changes to our manner of communications, creative approaches to doing business, and better leveraging of advanced technology have propelled us in such a way that bouncing back to normal is not an option.

A crisis, an unanticipated change, or even new conditions can take you to a point of no return. That is exactly what the 2020 pandemic did to us. It's similar to having an iPhone or Android and continuing to use a rotary dial telephone; failing to adapt to change will only leave you behind the curve. Adaptability must not be viewed as an effort to always return to normal, the old ways, or business as usual. Adaptability is the way we respond with resilience to keep performing, producing, and progressing forward.

Many experiments reveal quite a bit about aspects of human behavior, such as our resilience. In the 1980s, an experiment by psychologist Salvatore R. Maddi involved research into how we view stress and resilience. He conducted a study with 400 midlevel managers who faced job loss following the government breakup of AT&T in 1981. Questions arose concerning why two-thirds of the managers were falling apart from the stress of the company's reorganization, while the other third was surviving and thriving. It should not be surprising that their stress caused the larger group to suffer from heart attacks, strokes, depression, and drug abuse. He concluded that the third of the group was able to cope as a result of their attitude of commitment, control, and challenge under pressure. Their attitudes made the difference in not only their ability to survive, but also how they progressed.

Keep in mind that the experience these managers endured 40 years ago is still common today. Less than half of those with a similar experience were able to build up the resilience needed to face the disruption, which leads us to the importance of mindset.

Problematic Attitudes and Mindsets

All our actions trace back to our attitudes and mindsets. When we allow them to override how we respond to a situation, we limit our ability to adapt. Consider this quote from our favorite teenage surfer, Bethany Hamilton: "When you fall in the impact zone, get up, because you never know what's over the next wave." Or this one from Simon Sinek: "An infinite mindset sees opportunity in uncertainty." Mind over matter is more than just a saying.

A few common attitudes and mindsets inhibit our ability to respond positively to new circumstances. How often have you said or heard any of the following?

- "We've always done it that way."
- "This has worked for us for the last 30 years."
- "There's too much to learn if we go that route."
- "Let's just go back to what we were doing before."
- "Our clients are used to seeing the same things from us. They don't need anything different."

- "Trying something new is not a good idea."
- "Just hold on until we see better numbers."
- "I know the numbers look good for it, but that's not something we should try just yet."
- "Remember what happened to XYZ Company."
- "You don't want to end up like Will Winston when he tried a new idea."

I have heard almost all of these statements throughout my career. I can also admit that I have been guilty of using one when I was afraid of trying something new and different in order to respond to learners' changing needs in the workplace classroom. This self-reflection and self-awareness are key to improving your adaptability skills.

Many of these attitudes and mindsets stem from the fear of uncertainty, failure, or success. Yes, we can also fear success when we have an anxiety that something might really work and cause drastic change in our lives. It can be overwhelming for some to rise to the challenge of what is demanded.

These fears, resistances, and discomforts can make that comfort zone more enticing. And yet, our comfort zone might just be our downfall.

Leadership and Workplace Culture

Your company's leadership and the workplace culture that stems from what they signal as priorities can act as a barrier both to organizational and individual adaptability. Workplace culture is determined by the leadership's mindset, along with the workers, the work, the vision, and core values. Think about your workplace and its culture, as well as your organization's mission, vision, and values. If you know these off the top of your head, well done. If you can't, don't worry; you're in the majority—just look them up. Keep in mind, Patrick Lencioni (2002) explained that "values can set a company apart from the competition by clarifying its identity and serving as a rallying point for employees." What do these statements say about your business? Do yours suggest that your company values adaptability? Or do they project limitations on what you can do or accomplish in adapting as a team and company?

 Consider This

- What are your organization's mission, vision, and values?
- What do they say about the organization?
- Do suggest adaptability? Or do they project limitations?

Leadership sets the tone of workplace culture and whether innovation, creative thinking, critical thinking, and problem solving are promoted within it. Hearing these ideals reinforced in company communications, staff meetings, performance meetings, and in response to change indicates that they are recognized as key areas of the culture. A slow response, clinging to core revenue streams, short-term thinking, lack of process improvement, and prioritization of short-term profits are some ways your workplace might create barriers to adaptability. Recognizing past accomplishments and highlighting peak performance can be inspiring, but they should not be targets for a future destination, or become a blinding focus directing to the past rather than forward.

While adaptability is a skill, an organization can also enhance—or impede—individual and team adaptability through its processes. Not having an identified approach for the organization to adapt, having inconsistent approaches, or lacking leaders capable of implementing an approach can all overwhelm an individual's effort to be adaptable.

It's instructive to take a brief look at the way many successful organizations cycle through a general approach to adaptability. This will inform our focus in part 2 on how we put adaptability into practice, and you can use it as a benchmark to reflect on how your company adapts to change and where improvements can be made. I call it the FAST (flow of adaptability steps to take) Approach (Figure 3-1). As you review the steps, you

Figure 3-1. Flow of Adaptability Steps to Take (FAST) Approach to Organizational Adaptability

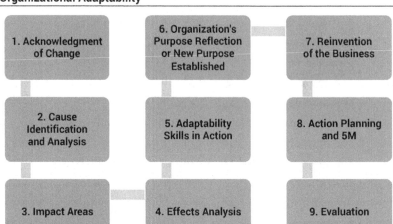

may identify some that you have seen completed in your organizations—or the lack thereof. The steps are:

1. Recognize and acknowledge the change that has taken place, and the new conditions. Examine what is and is not within the company's control.

2. Identify what things have happened internally and externally. In many instances, it may be relevant to research the cause of the change for future reference, to assist in problem solving, for planning purposes, and for managing risks.

3. Determine the areas of impact (business areas, products, services, staff, clients, technology, infrastructure, and so on).

4. Analyze the effects on the business, workplace, strategic plans, and operational goals.

5. Explore any areas of opportunity for creativity, innovation, collaboration, resilience, and flexibility. Gather the right people with an adaptability skill set and the company knowledge necessary to be effective and efficient in this step.

6. Make decisions, assess needs, and identify changes needed in vision, mission, strategic goals, values, operational plans, and partnerships.
7. Determine what to stop, start, or continue (business, marketing, products, services).
8. Create an adaptability action plan with 5M (machines, manpower, materials, methods, and money).
9. Establish an evaluation plan based on measurable business outcomes and a plan to monitor the progress. This answers the questions: Did it work? How did we do? Why or why not?

Steps in the FAST Approach are typically completed in the order shown. Depending on a company's size and intricacies, there may be additional steps between the ones provided. Based on the final step's results, it may be necessary to cycle back through the approach. Certain steps followed in your workplace, whether formal or informal, may align with the FAST Approach. Many organizations that are not successful in their adaptability approach may be challenged in the areas of capable staff, an effective process, response time, or functional leadership. But it's important to note: Change is not the reason for company failure—it is the unwillingness or incapability of leaders to cope with and respond to change.

⛯ Consider This

- What are examples of barriers you may not realize you are creating?
- What misconceptions are you correcting on adaptability?
- Are there distractions impeding your progress? If so, why?
- How can you improve the way you address your challenges and barriers?

Giving In to Distractions

Before we wrap up, it's important to address the elephant in the room when it comes to adaptability: giving in to distractions. In our tough times, with increased digitization and change, we have more distractions in the workplace that make it difficult to give our full attention. Udemy's *2018 Workplace Distraction Report* found that 61 percent of workers attribute workplace change to the high rate of distractions. And distractions can take all shapes and sizes: letting your attention wander to a big presentation you have to give later in the day when you are caught in an never-ending meeting, for example. Smaller but just as distracting are our phones and devices, with their constant notifications for texts, emails, or app updates. On an organizational level, getting caught up in the success of the moment with business booming is a typical distraction from a focus on the long term.

Have you ever taken your focus off your own aspiration momentarily when you heard about someone else receiving a job promotion? This distraction draws your attention away from focusing on how you can develop and adapt in the future. How about an excessive focus on something that you knew should have worked, but didn't? Being consumed by disappointment is a problem. Many personal situations present distractions that can influence judgment if you are not careful, because they can impede one's ability to be present in a situation. Distractions create interruptions that impede progress, inhibit problem resolution, camouflage issues, and kill productivity.

Overcoming Adaptability Barriers

From the individual to the business level, we need to address challenges and barriers to how we grow and adapt. Individually, we have to evaluate our mindsets in response to change. We must decide to let go without shutting down. At the workplace level, many see greater efficiency when the barriers to technology advancement are removed and they can accelerate task automation. At the organizational level, leadership must create a culture of innovation and remove constraints that impede creativity and innovation.

While the ways we adapt might vary, we all should expect change to occur rather than fighting or resisting it. We must learn to live with ambiguity and uncertainty and establish a response such as the FAST Approach when the need arises. Like a fire drill, your approach will prepare you with a lifesaving course of action, an escape plan, in the event of an emergency.

You may be starting to recognize the challenges and barriers you have encountered. The good news is that you are building up your body of knowledge so you can better respond. Think about other individuals who have this same knowledge, but whose actions don't reflect it. Part of the problem, rooted to a challenge or barrier, is with their learning agility. Many changes we experience will require something to be learned and something to be unlearned. Knowing when to do one versus the other factors into addressing the challenges and barriers to adapting.

The more I understood the ways I can be distracted, sidetracked, or discouraged personally and professionally, the more I recognized the value of adaptability. To master adaptability requires a bit of self-reflection and self-evaluation. I hope you are starting to recognize where you can exercise more of your potential based on your mindset and your view of challenges. In part 2, you'll begin to access the tools, approaches, and resources that can prepare you to face and respond to change and set you up for success in your AQ game.

PART 2
Putting Adaptability Into Practice

CHAPTER 4

Adaptability in Talent Development Is a Must

"Let us help you with your conversion to virtual." Less than 60 days following the start of the COVID-19 lockdown, this was the primary messaging for many organizations promoting their talent development services to potential clients. Instead of feeling like I wanted to scream with the next email solicitation or do a select all and delete, I realized that these organizations were doing what other organizations and talent development professionals needed to do.

Too many times we overlook the opportunities to practice what we teach. These individuals and businesses were:

- Responding to a crisis
- Pivoting in response to changing needs
- Focusing on future readiness and decision making
- Establishing a competitive advantage with a survival mindset
- Creating an opportunity
- Identifying their value proposition

If your organization was not shut down or left in limbo, then you were scurrying to adjust your workplace learning to meet the needs of a remote workforce. In my organization, our client companies were placing projects on hold, pulling the plug, or changing direction. Almost none of our clients were operating as usual. Contacts in my network were looking for resources on quick virtual conversion options for their in-person training programs.

Yet organizational talent development needs were beginning to multiply because of the work disruption even before the pandemic. The future of work, which already included the need to create and update remote work policies, required talent development to respond to the fast pace of business, new technologies, and increased demand for more engaging and personalized learning. Where is talent development headed, and what does it mean for talent development professionals who must learn to adapt? That is what we will discuss in the second part of this book, along with putting adaptability into practice.

A Historical View of Talent Development and ATD

Take a moment to consider how we define *talent development*. I like the ATD definition: "efforts that foster learning and employee development to drive organizational performance, productivity, and results." Talent development (TD) represents a profession in addition to a field of work (an area of focus that can represent various job roles extending beyond a single job title). As a field of work, talent development encompasses some common professions, including instructional designer, trainer, training coordinator, learning support specialist, performance consultant, e-learning developer, and TD director.

To arrive at this moment, the talent development industry has seen many evolutions to keep pace with changing needs, roles, and services. Consider how ATD, the largest association of talent development professionals in the world, has adapted to the times. With more than 75 years in existence, ATD has an established record for setting trends and best practices for talent development professionals to follow. One recent example was the transition it made from being the American Society for Training & Development to the Association for Talent Development in 2014. The name change was a response to industry changes to reflect the broad range of work roles within its membership. Today, talent development encompasses specialists, developers, curriculum architects, programmers, and other nontraditional talent development titles for those who hold field-related responsibilities.

My local chapter, ATD Detroit, took steps to communicate this change to our membership, but we also recognized the need to change how we served our members, as well as who we were targeting as members. Our board decided to include programming topics for those who were working in other roles but functioning as trainers or instructional designers. We also adjusted our membership and other promotional messages to include verbiage that was more inclusive. This aligned with what we were experiencing in some of our individual organizations as well. I had a greater respect and appreciation for ATD as well as my membership with the association, because it forced me to rethink my work and what I could contribute to my organization.

Workplace Evolutions and Adaptations

More vividly, talent development professionals can see beyond the individual level and take a look at how the workplace has evolved and adapted. The first Industrial Revolution and World War II helped to shape workplace learning in those times. Starting in the 1800s, machines in factories heightened the demand for factory workers to be trained. This resulted in classrooms being placed in factories, so companies could train multiple workers at one time with a single trainer. An even greater demand for large-group training came about with World War II, which also triggered a high volume of women to pursue jobs outside the home. Market expansion, factory sizes, production volume, and job growth were the types of changes we experienced. Workplace learning had to respond and adapt with more efficient training methods, lower training costs, industry-focused training, and individualized instruction.

Multiple factors have driven the modernization of workplace learning over the years. If we take a look back in history, we'll see a few vivid examples in the legislative domain. Following an economic downturn, the

Manpower Development and Training Act of 1962 enabled workers to receive necessary training and retraining as a result of automation and technological change. It was also an effort to combat rising unemployment while anticipating future needs for workplace learning. Does this sound similar to what happened when the COVID-19 pandemic started?

Formalized training became necessary with the establishment of official entities such as the Equal Employment Opportunity Commission (EEOC) in 1965 and the Occupational Safety and Health Administration (OSHA) in 1971. These organizations passed regulations that required employers to ensure that certain rights, such as a safe work environment, were upheld for employees. To do this, employers had to provide skills training in certain areas, which started changing the landscape of training and development in the workplace.

In 1990, the Americans With Disabilities Act (ADA) was signed into law, with the purpose of prohibiting discrimination against people with disabilities and ensuring that they are afforded the same opportunities as everyone else. Supervisors, managers, and others in the workforce had to be trained on the ADA. There were changes that had to be made within numerous organizations to ensure that workers with disabilities could receive certain training.

Here is another example that should be quite familiar to those who have some years in the game. During my time in city employment, I came across a number of documents referencing the personnel department. I recall asking what department that was, because I did not know there had been a department name change. Like in many other organizations in past years, the personnel department became the human resources department to reflect how its services had evolved, as well as the need to emphasize the human element. Established in the 1920s, personnel originally had a central focus on hiring, training, compensating, evaluating, and handling complaints. As business needs changed and evolved, the view of employees changed; they started to be seen as human assets who could affect business goals.

Major shifts in workplace learning over the years necessitated changes around training access, room layouts, technology, and audience. Training changed from push to pull accessibility. Before, employers pushed training to make it available when workers needed to know the information, or when training was required. Now, employees have training readily available for employees to pull when they want it. Room layouts were designed to accommodate more impactful learning, with group collaboration and teamwork. Whether it is instructor-led training, e-learning, or a virtual classroom, design has changed over the years to cater to the goals and tasks involved in the training. We've gone from in-person-only training with overhead projectors and transparencies to personalized learning, blended e-learning, or virtual reality simulations. And we now have five generations, from traditionalists to gen Z, making up today's diverse, multicultural workforce, which further emphasizes a need for our learning programs to be adaptable to the individual user.

New Capabilities for Talent Development Professionals

In 2020, ATD released its new Talent Development Capability Model, shown in Figure 4-1, replacing the ATD Competency Model. The Talent Development Capability Model presents a framework for the latest knowledge and skills that practitioners must have in talent development and represents where we are and where ATD sees the field going in the next few years. The model demonstrates ATD's future-focused work in setting a standard that can empower practitioners in our field. It also reiterates that being ready to adapt, whether it's for your career or the work you do on a daily basis, is an essential skill for talent development professionals.

The model organizes the 23 capabilities that practitioners in our field should have into three domains: Building Personal Capability, Developing Professional Capability, and Impacting Organizational Capability. By including personal skills and organizational knowledge, the model emphasizes that talent development professionals must show adaptability skills beyond their technical abilities.

Figure 4-1. Talent Development Capability Model

Building Personal Capability	Developing Professional Capability	Impacting Organizational Capability
• Communication • Emotional Intelligence & Decision Making • Collaboration & Leadership • Cultural Awareness & Inclusion • Project Management • Compliance & Ethical Behavior • Lifelong Learning	• Learning Sciences • Instructional Design • Training Delivery & Facilitation • Technology Application • Knowledge Management • Career & Leadership Development • Coaching • Evaluating Impact	• Business Insight • Consulting & Business Partnering • Organization Development & Culture • Talent Strategy & Management • Performance Improvement • Change Management • Data & Analytics • Future Readiness

Frequently, a contact will introduce me to someone who is trying to determine their next steps or create an action plan for their talent development career path. They may be recent college graduates, transitioning to talent development, or those with limited experience in the field. The Capability Model is a great tool for all of these people. You can reference the tool for skills, career steps for building experience, and action planning based on the capabilities. There are questions you can ask before embarking on a prescription. Regardless of your experience level, the model can provide guidance; it presents a starting point for some and a benchmark for others.

If you are familiar with the model, then you know that adaptability itself is not a capability it identifies. However, it is included, and here's how. Within the Building Personal Capability domain, you have the emotional intelligence and decision making capability, which has adaptability as part of it, as we explained in part 1. This domain also includes the Lifelong Learning capability, which covers self-motivation, curiosity, and risk-taking abilities.

In the Developing Professional Capability domain, technology selection and implementation is the ability to adapt and leverage certain technologies when needed for the organization. Designing, facilitating, and evaluating learning requires technology to some degree. Our jobs involve keeping current with technology to achieve this in the most creative, efficient, and innovative ways possible.

In the final domain, Impacting Organizational Capability, we have consulting and business partnering, with a focus on facilitating change and improvement in the business. Another capability for this domain is business insight. Being adaptable means recognizing industry influences and understanding what affects business growth.

Let me offer my perspective of the model and where I stand. Naturally, there are capabilities that I need to acquire or enhance. Personally, the capabilities that captured my attention were cultural awareness and inclusion, evaluating impact, business insight, and future readiness. They helped me realize how much I needed to level up, because they were not areas I'd targeted for my development. The model helped me to see that they are important now and in the future. Cultural awareness and inclusion is not just a trend; diversity and inclusion (D&I) and diversity, equity, and inclusion (DEI) are hot topics. Yes, it's the hard target for a diversity awareness training or an employee engagement initiative. However, how do I represent cultural awareness and inclusion in a leadership development program, mentoring program, or employee retention initiative?

Evaluating impact should be taken beyond the work we may do just shy of Kirkpatrick Levels 3 and 4. How are you taking your evaluation approach and strategy to new heights to better align your training initiatives with business results?

Earlier in my career, I mistakenly saw business insight and future readiness as areas for upper management. This type of mindset just won't cut it for today's talent development professional. Even in an entry-level role, you need to consider your organization's growth as you factor in how the company spends money and makes money. We should not be so engrossed in our own worlds or individual roles that business insight and future readiness have no relevance.

You may have your own aha moment about the model. You may see that it doesn't just stop at your areas of strength or those in which the majority of your work takes place, but that it ventures into capabilities to which you may have given a back seat.

 Consider This
- In what ways am I learning, unlearning, and relearning to build upon the roots applicable to my work as a talent development professional?
- Where do I see opportunity to apply a more forward-thinking mindset to my talent development practices?

DEI in Talent Development

Parts of this book were written during the year following the killing of George Floyd on May 25, 2020, by a Minneapolis police officer. The video of the officer pinning Floyd to the ground for more than eight minutes by kneeling on his neck (an action that was ultimately fatal) sparked a renewed movement for social justice and protests against inequality and racism. It forced us to see how much we still needed to work toward DEI on the individual, organizational, and societal levels, including the need to unlearn poor behaviors and learn healthy ones, become curious about other cultures and promote collaboration, appreciate differences, improve interpersonal communications, and most prominent—manage our emotions with unplanned change. I believe these reflect DEI's roots in adaptability.

However, before the work can be done it's important to understand what DEI means:

- **Diversity** is the presence of visible and invisible differences among people, including race, gender, age, religion, sexual orientation, ethnicity, nationality, socioeconomic status, disability, or social differences.
- **Inclusion** is when we create an environment where people feel welcome, valued, and a sense of belonging.
- **Equity** is ensuring that everyone has equal access to opportunities and resources for everyone.

According to a McKinsey report, culturally diverse companies experience 36 percent greater profitability than other companies (Dixon-Fyle et al. 2020). We also see how important TD professionals are in strategizing, partnering with business areas, sponsoring communication efforts that give workers a voice, providing DEI training at all levels of the organization, and sharing best practices for recruiting diverse talent. Think about the ways you have already and still need to incorporate DEI in your personal and professional life.

Leaders and workers are not oblivious to the growing demand for DEI work. Attendees at my presentations are increasingly asking how to encourage resistant leaders to make DEI a priority, as well as if I can provide examples of actionable DEI steps, discuss the importance of psychological safety, and share how to start employee resource groups (ERGs). DEI topics of interest will likely change as we experience more marginal impact, which means that we need to continue our professional development in cultural awareness.

Being a Talent Development Professional Means Adapting

Drilling down from the industry level, how has the profession itself adapted and evolved over time? Nearly 60 years ago, Malcolm Knowles introduced andragogy, based on adult-learning principles. Based on these principles, adults need:

- Self-directed learning
- Learning that is relevant to prior knowledge and experiences
- Learning that is applicable to real-life tasks or problems for immediate application
- To be respected in their readiness to learn
- To know the goal or reason for learning something
- To be intrinsically motivated to learn

These adult-learning principles form the foundation of talent development today and allow us to adapt as technology advances and research reveals new insights. Our roots give us a firm grounding for our growth potential when we exercise agility to unlearn and relearn as needed. In my early days as an instructional designer and a trainer, I had a colleague who was opposed to many of my instructional methodologies, some of which had participants move around the room, play games, or use toys to facilitate learning. Despite being the youngest trainer on the training team, I tried not to take it personally, especially when I saw how much participants enjoyed my courses based on evaluation feedback and returning participants. My colleague's belief was that I only wanted to play games, and that professional development is not supposed to be fun.

The interesting part was that I was generating these ideas from my research and what I was learning from those who were recognized in the field, such as Bob Pike in his "Creative Training Techniques" newsletter, Kirkpatrick's Four Levels of Evaluation, and ATD's *TD at Work*. I was learning to build upon my foundational knowledge of andragogy and its adult-learning principles. I wanted to apply techniques and ideas in a way that represented my style, expertise, and passion. I did not allow resistance or opposition to my ideas to deter me. My agenda was to design innovative, creative, and impactful learning experiences. Through my commitment to lifelong learning, I tapped into my adaptability skills to offer the best talent development programs possible. Although we do not have one single theory to explain adult learning, theories like andragogy reflect how we can continue to adapt learning practices to research and new insights to guide workplace learning strategy.

We have been on a roller-coaster ride with talent development that started long before COVID-19. The changes we are implementing will certainly outlive the pandemic. In the rest of this chapter, I want to highlight a few of the areas in our talent development practice where adaptability is a must. We'll focus on the shift to e-learning and virtual training, developing remote workforces, adapting to learner-driven learning, and social learning.

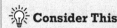 **Consider This**
- How am I diversifying my skill set to promote my adaptability?
- How am I improving my technological savvy to enhance my adaptability and agility?

E-Learning and Virtual Learning

As early as 2003, e-learning accounted for 3 percent of learning hours, while in 2018, 42 percent of learning hours were technology-based (Sugrue and Rivera 2005; ATD 2019). In 2002, only 15 percent of delivery methods involved learning technologies; by 2019, it had almost tripled, to 43 percent. ATD's *2020 State of the Industry* report found that self-paced e-learning accounted for 26 percent of the training hours that organizations provided to employees, while virtual classrooms accounted for 19 percent. Report updates for 2020 are likely to show nearly double the 2019 results because of COVID-19.

More and more organizations are offering e-learning to employees. Employees can do it when it is convenient for them, and at their own pace. This learning is easily tracked, which makes it ideal for compliance and other mandated training. E-learning's improved adaptive learning and personalization features also make it more ideal for organizations to invest in. For example, it may be more feasible to update a policy or replace images to reflect a diverse audience in an e-learning course than to revise multiple materials in different places for a traditional ILT program.

Technology's accessibility has allowed e-learning, virtual reality, and machine learning to grow in popularity for talent development in recent years. Our work promotes continued efforts to improve learning experiences, increase the volume of learners, make content more digestible, improve efficiency, provide L&D metrics, and achieve business results.

Unfortunately, the fear of technology or resistance to its use can impede adaptability, progress, and even survival. I have seen this with organizations, leaders, and workers who find learning new technology to be too time-consuming, overwhelming, or uncomfortable. I had initial fears when learning to connect my phone to my car through Bluetooth, using an ATM for the first time, or setting up a programmable thermostat in my home. However, I did not permit those fears to restrain me from learning something that would increase efficiency in some way and enhance my quality of life. Technology can improve our quality of life along with our work efficiency if we get out of our comfort zones. It's called change, and it happens voluntarily and involuntarily, just like our adaptability at times.

Remote Work

Before the pandemic and certainly since, organizations have had to determine remote-work policies: how to continue work operations, how to supervise remote work, how to communicate with remote workers, how to promote employee engagement, how to address employee problems, and how to provide training for it all. For my organization, it was not a major adjustment, because working from home was a part of our business culture, we had a policy in place, and our talent development was primarily e-learning. Despite this, we had to change how we conducted internal meetings, the way we communicated work updates, and the focus of the business. I had contacts in my network, leaders within their organizations, who were not in the same position as us. They had to quickly make some major decisions in their organizations. Later mandates for social distancing, mask wearing, and crowd limitations added to an already overwhelming situation for many organizational leaders. For others, these were driving forces to identify ways to adapt the business. With business limitations resulting in customer declines, adapting required innovative and creative thinking along with decision making.

It was apparent to organizations that they needed to find better ways to leverage technology to meet their talent development needs. Virtual was the optimal answer for many industries. With this type of innovation, workplace learning would have a stake in the game at some point to help workers acclimate to the technology, learn a new system, implement process change, and adhere to new safety guidelines.

To those organizations that failed to think in terms of how to adapt, the options for workplace learning seemed limited. Going virtual and digital was the best approach, and that remains the case today. During my presidency, our ATD Detroit Chapter went predominantly virtual by offering monthly webinars and only several in-person events in 2019. This was a strategic decision for us to improve our chapter membership and program attendance. Little did we know that our strategic change would be a saving grace in 2020. Organizations with the technological resources and a culture acclimated to virtual and digital learning had an advantage like our chapter. Workplace learning had to be a priority for the organization's survival.

Innovative approaches to workplace learning have changed the way we design and offer training, curriculums, and learning options to address skills gaps and development. The traditional practice of scheduling courses, marketing them in the organization, and conducting them in-person may soon be a distant memory. An initial step for organizations is identifying the training topics to target for development based on job roles, work, identified capabilities, and organizational goals. Another step is determining the budget, the technology available, and internal resources. Regardless of what was done previously, these are two steps learning leaders needed to revisit once COVID-19 hit.

Adjusting to remote work, virtual meetings, and a greater dependence on technology became additional areas to address for workplace learning that were not priorities previously. Considering this, we can see how Zoom, Webex, and GotoWebinar quickly rose in popularity as technology options for virtual meetings; likewise, LinkedIn Learning quickly became a popular learning resource. More major steps for learning leaders involved quickly locating resources for off-the-shelf training or converting internal training to e-learning options, ensuring the availability and accessibility of the required technology, and determining the messaging for promoting the training to staff. A few of our client organizations shared that they were forced to take these steps as they worked to adapt.

Learner-Driven Learning

Learner-driven experiences are becoming more prevalent with technological and societal disruptions. Workers expect the same convenience from workplace learning as they do in their personal lives. Consider the growing popularity of BOPIS (buy online, pick up in-store) as a shopper-driven experience. Risley (2020) shared that BOPIS increased by more than 500 percent in April 2020. Shoppers can get what they want when they want it. In a similar respect, learners can also have more control over their learning experience thanks to technology. Workers may be encouraged to take charge of their own learning path with minimal guidance to get them started, due to limited resources within the organization. Making performance support tools accessible to workers at the moment of need provides another reason for promoting the learner-driven experience.

Promotion of a learner-driven experience can depend on an organization's budget. There are numerous off-the-shelf options, but general topics such as change management, conflict management, diversity awareness, emotional intelligence, leadership development, and team building are available for free or at a low cost. When consulting with clients on ways to diversify their workplace learning using current technology, I recommend e-learning, webinars, blogs, tutorials, job aids, VILT, podcasts, and TED Talks. This list continues to grow as we experience more technological advancements. With any budget, an organization can apply an adaptable approach to its workplace learning and experience success with the necessary innovation and decision making put into a well-structured plan.

Social Learning

Have you ever wondered about the power behind an individual sharing an experience with a peer and how this influences learning? Thanks to Albert Bandura (1977), we have a greater respect for peer collaboration. According to his social learning theory, observing and modeling the behavior of others in a social context is a way of learning. However, Bandura explains that we can't learn simply by observing someone perform a behavior, conditions require us to be mentally ready to learn.

The value of social learning is not limited to talent development because it is something we have been doing since childhood. Demos of people modeling behaviors are common in podcasts, videos, microlearning, and other modes, which are excellent examples of how to leverage social learning. In my courses I like to share problems or challenges I've faced and then discuss how I resolved or overcame it. This is one way that we engage in social learning for others.

You can use social learning to help grow your adaptability skills and further your research. In chapter 8, we'll discuss how to make it a part of your development path.

A Cue for High AQ

ATD's Talent Development Capability Model highlights a variety of areas that should capture our attention in our efforts to identify where and how we put adaptability to work. Learning the ways to put AQ to work and continuing to excel at it can position you for high-AQ status. Your work is cut out for you in adapting to present circumstances along with what's to come, which may include initiating needed changes.

CHAPTER 5

Adaptability's Value Proposition

"It was the best of times, it was the worst of times, it was the age of wisdom, it was the age of foolishness." Charles Dickens wrote in *A Tale of Two Cities*. We often hear this classic reference used to depict two opposing perspectives of a situation. I see how this applies to our experience with COVID-19. Times seemed at their worst with regulations, mandates, restrictions, and limitations. At the same time, we were able to exercise a resilience to achieve greatness with new inventions, creations, ideas, and innovations. If you can see the best of times in the midst of the worst of times, you have something to distinguish yourself from others. You have a value proposition.

What Value Do You Provide?

In the worst of times, it might be the best time for talent development professionals like us to distinguish ourselves through our adaptability. We can do that by defining our value proposition, which shows what makes you unique and why you stand above the rest. When you explain why someone should hire you, promote your training program, or persuade someone to use your training services, you are stating your value proposition. If you do not see value in what you do, bring, or contribute, then it is unlikely that anyone else will. Your value proposition should be a stable element in your career strategy.

The opportunity presented for us as talent development professionals to distinguish ourselves is becoming more evident. Leaders must rethink how their organizations create value in uncertain times, and talent development professionals have a responsibility to do something similar. According to Jim Collins (2001), "The good-to-great companies understood that doing what you are good at will only make you good; focusing solely on what you can potentially do better than any other organization is the only path to greatness." It is about making your mark and making it known with your value proposition.

Your value comes from those things that are unique to your style, service, product, or passion. When people get you, what exactly are they getting? In my last month as the ATD Detroit chapter president, I attended a session that walked me through steps to answer that question. The ATD Chicagoland chapter was hosting a conference, and one of the sessions was about determining your value proposition. Hayward Suggs, president-elect for ATD Chicagoland, had us consider using an elevator speech to communicate our value proposition as a way to quickly capture the listener's attention. First, we identified the pain points for the prospective client. Next, we asked them a question related to their pain points. Then, we stated our value proposition.

Here is how an example of this might sound. Let's say that my prospective client has problems getting their leaders to think outside the box. Once I learn what their pain point is, I can use the following approach: "How would you like to get your leaders to think outside the box in a way that causes your company to thrive in obtaining business results? I am a 'people potential accelerator,' and I facilitate a webinar for this—'The Fast and Furious Drive to Adaptability.' Here is my contact information, and I would be happy to share more when you have time."

Prior to this exercise, I did not appreciate the importance of establishing and communicating your value proposition. Since that 2019 conference session, my opinion of a value proposition has been that you have a problem if you don't have one for yourself. Your value proposition should function as your point of return or foundation, because it presents your package labeling in a sense. It's a synopsis of your value and what you bring to the table.

As trainers, instructional designers, project managers, and presenters, we must recognize the value we bring and the role adaptability plays in our work. Take the time to determine your value proposition and write it down. Misconceptions about the value proposition result in people creating a simple catchphrase, slogan, or tag line. If you are wondering where you should begin, apply these steps in formulating a draft of your value proposition. It should include a headline, sub headline or paragraph, three to five bullets (optional), and a visual cue. Follow these steps and use the questions listed to guide you.

Writing Your Value Proposition

1. Start with your why:
   ◦ Why do you exist?
   ◦ What are your vision and mission?
   ◦ What are your values?
2. Define your product, service, or idea with an accurate description:
   ◦ What do you provide?
   ◦ How does your product (service, idea, and so on) work?
3. Identify all the benefits that your product, service, or idea provides:
   ◦ Why should the customer care?
   ◦ How will your solution benefit your customers?
4. Express these benefits in quantifiable value:
   ◦ What value can customers expect to receive?
   ◦ What is the value of your individual selling points?
5. Identify your customers' pain points:
   ◦ What issues do they have?
   ◦ What keeps your customers up at night?
6. Connect the value to the customers' pain points:
   ◦ How can you solve your customers' problems or issues?
   ◦ When and how will the customers recognize the value?

7. Differentiate yourself from the competition:
   - Why should customers choose you over the competition?
   - What is unique about what you offer?
8. Determine a strategy for communicating your value proposition:
   - How will you share your value proposition with your target audience (customers and potential customers)?
   - What communication modes should be leveraged?

Making Adaptability Part of Your Value Proposition

We've established that creating your value proposition is a foundational success factor for you as a talent development professional. I want to connect that to assessing your adaptability skills. The needs of organizations, teams, and learners continue to change. As leaders rethink how their organizations create value in uncertain times, your value as a talent development professional lies in your adaptability skills and ability to lead the organization through uncertainty.

Reflect on your thoughts, behaviors, and practices. Think about the ways you are changing to meet those needs. You need adaptability skills to recognize changes, respond to them, and get leadership on board with your approach. Your AQ can determine how successful you are at this.

Think about this example. Prior to COVID-19, I was somewhat of an avid cruiser, with seven or so cruises under my belt. A few of them were deals I could not refuse. Hurricane season is generally from June to November, and the deals for that time were very enticing. Let's use this as an analogy to storms or crises in business. High-AQ individuals are an asset to their organizations in helping them prepare for storms in non-storm seasons. They are not quick to panic when a storm arises. Alternatively, they follow the contingency plan and may test things that were not in the plan to see if they will work. They can make hard decisions promptly without being emotionally driven.

Regardless of the season, cruise ships prepare for storms or emergencies as well. Before a cruise ship sets sail with passengers, there is always a muster drill (also known as a lifeboat drill) so that everyone gathers at the same time and knows what to do in an emergency. You may be surprised to know that the *Titanic* had one scheduled for the day it sank, but it was canceled. Even during an enjoyable experience, you need to be prepared for change or a crisis.

Adaptability should be part of the value proposition for all talent development professionals. The work we do is about training and development for leaders and workers in the areas of knowledge, skills, attitude, and behavior to meet organizational goals. I think we can find ourselves too entrenched in tradition, and thus limit our creative thinking and innovation. We tend to become too relaxed and fail to explore beyond what we are currently doing. "All of this sounds good," you might be thinking, "but in reality, we do not have time for creativity, design thinking, innovation, problem solving, and other adaptability-related efforts." This is part of the initiative required on our end to see how we can build this into our current workloads. Do you schedule time for brainstorming, creative thinking, problem solving, or innovation? Is there opportunity to reduce time in other areas to allow time for these adaptability efforts? More than ever before, we are positioned to leverage technology to enhance our value to organizations, but it takes action on our part without waiting for the organization to make it happen.

 Consider This

- How can I distinguish my skills, experience, and talents to create a value proposition?
- In the Talent Development Capability Model, which capabilities are my strengths and which are my opportunities?

Gig Economy

Crossroads of changing work, performance expectations, value proposition, and autonomous working arrangements have launched us into an explosion of the gig economy—and it's no longer a new job market. Freelancers and independent workers represent the gig economy. Having a gig has become the ideal option for those who have the drive to make use of their skills—instead of holding a permanent role with one organization, people can take on temporary, on-call, or contract work. Today employers often hire gig workers rather than a full-time employee to complete a job. In fact, approximately 30 percent of US workers are part of the gig economy, according to 2018 Gallup research. This is expected to increase by more than 50 percent of US workers by 2027 (Deloitte 2017). We can expect laws and regulations pertaining to gig workers to adapt to the changes we are seeing in the traditional employment model.

Some people question whether the gig economy is friend or foe. The answer would likely depend on whom you ask. The gig economy affords employers and workers a level of flexibility and freedom. Work-life balance is a major feature of its appeal. Despite challenges that accompany the rising gig economy, it leaves us hungry for adaptability in many ways. Challenges are decentralization, less cohesion on a team, and training. L&D is a key resource in designing the level of training an organization has to provide its gig workers. Some other training areas are the engagement and integration of gig workers with full-time workers in an organization.

Your AQ Story

What's your adaptability story? Everyone has one. The question is whether yours tells the story of a high-adaptability individual. Are you receptive to unplanned change? How do you demonstrate resilience and flexibility? Are you willing to try new things and listen with an open mind? Have you started a gig or thought about how to tap into your value proposition to get one going? Throughout our work and personal lives, we communicate our adaptability.

Within your organization, you can demonstrate high-adaptability skills by sharing ideas, taking the initiative, and contributing to team development. We have to be willing to learn, unlearn, and relearn the right things at the right time. Each time I have learned a new tool for developing e-learning or project management, I find the need to relearn and sometimes unlearn in order to accommodate new information. There are times when you need to lean backward as you lean forward.

You need to be a hunter-gatherer. You need to be on the hunt for the experiences, lessons learned, and opportunities that show off your strong adaptability skills. You also need to gather adaptability achievements by reflecting on your past adaptability-related behaviors, thinking about steps you have taken to adapt in different situations, and assessing your adaptability in general. Previous promotions and increased responsibility in your career progression can indicate your ability to adapt to major changes and take on challenges. Then you can collect what you have learned about yourself to create your adaptability story.

Over the course of writing this book, I've reflected on the situations that challenged my resilience, such as my layoff nearly a decade ago and being asked to assume roles for special projects. I've thought about times when I took on difficult challenges and was innovative to locate solutions.

For example, nearly 20 years ago, I remember being part of the project team that handled my company's recognition and professional development conference. I was a new instructional designer and trainer assisting with a one-day event for a couple hundred internal staff and maybe one or two breakout sessions. Because of my desire to develop my skills outside my degree programs, I attended workshops and conferences regularly. I was always looking to apply what I learned in my role with my organization. I did this with the conference, which I took over from someone else. Each year for the three years I managed this conference project, one important goal for me was to create a recognition and development experience that was better for attendees than the previous year. In my final year with that organization, my project team and I were able to grow the event to more than 300 attendees, with presenters donating their time for 14 breakout sessions covering personal and professional topics and a vendor expo. This was a result of my exposure and keeping my vision stronger than my memory of what was done in the past so I could add value.

Another example is from about seven years ago. I was chaperone for a student exchange group traveling to Japan for a few weeks. I saw this as an opportunity to apply my cultural experience, work with diverse groups, and collaborate with foreign leadership, since we met with two mayors and one city council during our time there. Creating the picture for your AQ story helps you to identify your accomplishments and opportunities for development.

Think back to the value proposition I asked you to jot down earlier. Does that reflect your ability to adapt, respond to change, and embrace uncertainty?

 Consider This
- Who needs to know my value proposition and when should I communicate it?
- What is my AQ story?
- What steps can I take to assess and reveal my AQ?

Tools to Assess Your Current Adaptability Skills

"Adapt or die" can be taken seriously in business, so tools for assessing one's AQ measure should be factored into your decision to upgrade your adaptability skills. How often do you find yourself saying that you are improving in a given area or skill, but you do not have a way of identifying your exact status or how you measure up against a certain standard? A good idea would be finding out how you rank when it comes to AQ, because it's not easily determined by reflecting on your habits and behaviors alone. When we think about a test or measure, you can use the results to find out where you are and how far you need to go to reach a certain goal.

You might be familiar with the tools for measuring EQ; the same tools apply to AQ. Tools range from the fairly simple to the extremely complex. Those on the simple side apply a Likert scale to response items for completion. At the more complex end, Paul Stoltz (2019) has an AQ assessment based on four subscales that make up your CORE. The CORE of your AQ consists of:

- **Control**: your perception of your ability to improve a situation
- **Ownership**: your perception of your responsibility and accountability to improve an adverse situation
- **Reach**: your perception of scope of the adverse situation affecting other areas of your life
- **Endurance**: your perception of how long the adverse situation will last

He also describes these subscales as dimensions, which are similar to the four quadrants in Daniel Goleman's EQ Model. Stoltz designed several other tools that you will find in his book *Adversity Quotient @ Work*. Select a tool that can give you actionable results.

A Path to Development

You have to know your worth as well as your place in talent development. "Knowing your place" is something you might hear a person of age express to a youth who is talking or acting out of turn. In this instance, I mean it in a way that provokes a talent development professional to step up and seize the moment: addressing workforce learning pain points, questioning if one's organization is training to its greatest potential, keeping learning relevant to meet current workplace needs, or moving the organization in the direction of the future of work. If there is a problem related to training, performance improvement, organization development, or adaptability, are you waiting to get a tap on the shoulder, or do you have your hand raised to respond or act? Exhibiting confidence in knowing and taking your place is required for others to recognize you. It is also an aspect of adaptability, because you are taking the initiative to address situations, solve problems, and make decisions. That is a quality of someone whom many want to have on their team, especially in tough times. I see where I fit into this picture, and you should, too. We are the problem solvers with a persistence in getting to the root of L&D problems and arriving at a creative and innovative solution.

That is another advantage with using the Talent Development Capability Model as a resource; it will to help you determine your place inside and outside the organization. Application of the model leaves us without an excuse for what we should know and do in our field, and your value proposition is a by-product. In chapter 4, we also discussed the roots of adult learning. The model highlights adult-learning theories, foundational theories, and other learning sciences that we must incorporate into learning programs. You can't incorporate what you don't know. We are responsible for our ongoing development as lifelong learners, continuing to adapt in our work to achieve our own performance improvement in addition to that of the organization's workforce. Make your adaptability efforts count in ways with identifiable value for your organization, using the Talent Development Capability Model as part of your approach. You'll be glad you did.

CHAPTER 6

Build an Adaptive Mindset

If you ask someone who they believe is the pioneer of the personal computer, Steve Jobs would likely be a common answer. Jobs was one of the original masterminds behind the creation of Apple in 1976, which grew to be worth almost $1 million in 1980. Despite the growing success, Apple's board decided to remove Jobs because of poor business decisions and internal disagreements over future direction, leading to his resignation in 1985. His leadership qualities also contributed to the decline in the number of people who favored him.

Jobs found that his next role needed to include a change in his attitude and mindset. He worked on developing his leadership skills, because he recognized that to be better, we must do better once we think better. Here was a tech giant who believed that he could still make a comeback after a great fall. He maintained a belief in his vision, himself, and what the right people on his team could achieve, as well as a deep love for his work. These beliefs inspired him to move from a public seat of shame with the job loss to a private seat of a success seeker with his fresh start.

Jobs boasted that leaving the company turned out to be one of the best things that ever happened to him. After leaving Apple, Jobs started the NeXT company, which would be Apple's saving grace. In 1997, Apple purchased NeXT and Jobs returned as CEO of Apple; at the time, Apple was in financial distress and needed him. From his return until he stepped down in 2011 for health reasons, he helped lead Apple to become one of the most famous and trusted companies in the world. The same person it pushed out was being pulled back, thanks to his self-awareness, his change in attitude, and his ability to learn from his mistakes.

Determine Your Self-Awareness

As you might recall from earlier in the book, self-awareness is a key component to developing your emotional intelligence. It is also essential for building the mindset to adapt to whatever change or challenge you face in talent development.

To raise your self-awareness and improve your adaptability, you can use a tool called the Johari window. Maybe a year into my career, I was tasked with redesigning a diversity awareness course. Using the Johari window was one way I applied adaptability in redesigning the course. I added group discussion questions and an activity I created to connect the Johari window to diversity and promote awareness. You could say that I applied creativity and innovation by including the Johari window, along with implementing an activity to make it diversity focused.

Critical thinking, collaboration, and positivity were more skills I applied during the redesign using the Johari window tool. I used critical thinking to align the application exercises to course goals while ensuring they could allow for engagement and interaction. Critical thinking was also important for identifying potential participant feedback with topic discussions. I collaborated with peers on our training team for ideas and feedback on how I wanted to implement the tool. Positivity also factors in when you think about potential ways to combat negative situations with participants who are reluctant to be transparent or with those who go too far and share too much. I depended on my positivity skills to identify facilitation techniques when this happens.

The story we tell about ourselves may not match the story someone tells about us based on their impression of us as an individual, team member, or leader. The Johari window helps to explain why. There are four quadrants, or panes, that represent an overall view of the individual

(Figure 6-1). We tend to overlook the differences between how we see ourselves and the way others see us. By increasing what is known about ourselves and others and decreasing what is not known, we can improve our own awareness as well as that in our interpersonal relationships. The goal is to increase this arena awareness ("open area"), and is part of the reason behind the "window" portion of the name. Using this model assists with building trust and increasing self-awareness, which are both needed in adaptability.

Figure 6-1. The Johari Window

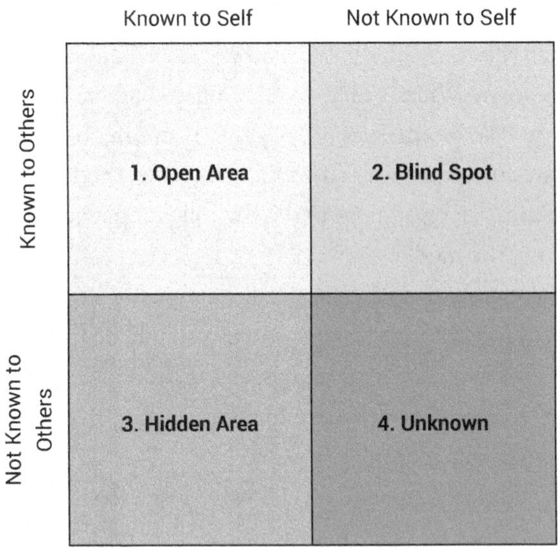

	Known to Self	Not Known to Self
Known to Others	1. Open Area	2. Blind Spot
Not Known to Others	3. Hidden Area	4. Unknown

Let's walk through each of the four quadrants:

1. **Open area:** Behaviors, traits, motives, attitudes, skills, and knowledge of an individual known to them and others.
   - *Example:* You are a previous business owner with a strong entrepreneurial spirit, and you are big on taking risks. Although your business did not succeed, everyone knows you are not afraid to step out with an idea.

2. **Blind spot:** What others perceive about you, but you don't realize about yourself.
   ○ *Example:* You are not aware of your low EQ and your limited ability to empathize with others, but others know this about you, especially when you are facilitating your courses.
3. **Hidden area:** The state of an individual known to them but not to others. This may be characteristic of introverts, who are not inclined to share their thoughts, feelings, or ideas with others.
   ○ *Example:* You have a high level of adaptability when it comes to adverse situations, and you realize this. However, others on your team are not aware of what you can do, because you are fairly new.
4. **Unknown:** What is unknown to you and others about yourself.
   ○ *Example:* Suppressed or forgotten memories of past experiences.

There are some dots we can connect between the Johari window and your adaptability development path. The following approach can be used when applying the model:

1. Focus on the open area as the optimal public area for good communication and cooperation. It should be free of mistrust, confusion, misunderstandings, and distractions, which can hinder high-adaptability skill development along with others' perceptions of your adaptability skills.
2. Ask for and be open to receiving feedback from others to reduce your blind spot while increasing the open area. Solicit feedback so you are aware of the views others have of you.
3. Disclose (as appropriate) more about you to those at work to reduce the hidden area. Sensitivities, fears, and hidden agendas are examples of what can be disclosed.
4. Discover more about yourself through feedback, reflection, and discussion. Make use of coaching and counseling opportunities to uncover hidden talents, repressed feelings, and traumatic past experiences.

With increased self-awareness, you are now primed to consider how you can change your attitude to one that embraces adaptability and doesn't shy away from change.

Change Your Attitude

"You really need to fix your attitude." Has someone ever told you this, and did you do it? Why or why not? There is a saying, "You cannot control what happens to you, but you can control your attitude toward what happens to you, and in that, you will be mastering change, rather than allowing it to master you."

Your actions tell onlookers much about your attitude in the midst of change. How often do you reflect on your own attitude instead of waiting for feedback from someone else? There is always room for improvement, and your attitude is no exception. This was true for me when I was laid off years ago and again when I was job searching during the 2020 COVID-19 pandemic. These were two pivotal points when I was on the brink of throwing my hands up and questioning what I was doing with my skills, education, talent, and life. Almost 10 years separated these events. For some, they might seem to be no big deal, but it's different when you are in the situation and your attitude can make or break you. I needed an attitude adjustment in adapting to these changes, which resulted in being able to obtain leadership and management job roles.

Checking your attitude is something that is easier said than done. Your attitude is the way you feel or act based your experience and temperament. Many of us believe that we have the right attitude until we face a change that catches us off guard. Do you try to excuse your attitude in the moment and place the blame on the situation to justify your inability to cope? That is a clear indicator that we have some work to do in developing our adaptability.

In *No Limits*, Maxwell (2017) said that your attitude alone does not sum up what you need in life, but it sets the tone for it. He explained three truths that we must recognize and say aloud:

- "I need to change." (I need to do this for me.)
- "I'm able to change." (I can achieve this and it's realistic.)
- "I'll be rewarded for change." (I will see a benefit with the outcome of the change.)

Once you say something out loud to yourself, it makes it real and promotes a greater self-commitment, which we will deal with later in this book.

We need to work on how we handle these truths as shared by Maxwell. The first truth requires detachment from deniability. This begins with the diagnosis of the problem or gap in your attitude. Improvements needed in my attitude and situation became evident in this step.

⌁ Consider This

- What do you realize that you need to change about your attitude?
- In what areas do you struggle with recognizing what is actually in your control?

The second truth is understanding what you can control. If you can change it, then you have control over it. This became real to me when deciding to become an ATD chapter board member, pursue my doctoral degree, and seek higher-level talent development roles. Think about decisions you can make to improve your situation when facing the need to adapt.

The final truth is about what you are able to envision for yourself. Great visionaries can build up expectations to be seen beyond the current circumstances. Why can't that be you? You need the right mindset and attitude to affect the desired results. Apply a future focus to create a vision of what you have the capability to be and do without allowing your current work situation or circumstances to distract you. I know my truth, and hopefully you are learning and handling yours; it should sound a lot like adaptability.

Here's an exercise with questions you can ask about your attitude toward building an adaptive mindset:

- **Detach from deniability:** What is one example of a truth you no longer deny about your attitude (such as lack of optimism, thinking the worst rather than the best, holding grudges)?
- **Grasp what you can control:** What is an example of a personal or professional situation you have the power to change (such as a decision you can make, an action you can take, or someone you can contact)?
- **Envision the future:** What is an example of a vision you have beyond what the current circumstances in relation to your job, your career, your business, your education, your health, your family, or something else?

Let's touch on control for a moment. One challenge for many of us is the ability to distinguish between and accept what we can and cannot control. This is captured in the serenity prayer: "God grant me the serenity to accept the things I cannot change, the courage to change the things I can, and the wisdom to know the difference."

Control is often a part of our struggle, and that influences our adaptability. We overlook what's within our control and focus excessively on what's outside our control. The areas of development we can identify are our recognition of what we can control, how we handle areas of control, and the way we respond to what is outside our control. This is the case when you have a meltdown because someone rejects your idea, hires another candidate instead of you, or doesn't appear to like you.

Back in 1986, R&B artist Janet Jackson released her *Control* album and put the spotlight on our desire to have it. This was her third album and was considered both evolutionary and revolutionary as a breakthrough for her professionally and personally. She evolved with this album by coming out of the shadows, sharing her true gifts, and expressing who she wanted to be moving forward. This paved the way for her to influence the work of other artists and achieve her first record-breaking album. The same applies to what we may find ourselves doing in talent development roles. Our attitude and skill development can help us achieve success in this endeavor. Getting to the heart of the matter is one way to develop your control. We reach a crossroads where we have to choose to evolve, to embrace change, or to shift to a new normal.

Learn From Your Mistakes and Failures

I see some of my mistakes as missed moments of adaptability. You might ask why I say that. Mistakes can be those situations where you failed to apply some aspect of adaptability and it led to a failure or an unsuccessful outcome. About two years into my role as a training specialist in the HR department, my training manager asked if I was interested in doing a job rotation throughout our nine department divisions. In this rotation, I would keep my training title but would fill a role in each division for a period of time and learn about its function, processes, and learning needs. This would have allowed me to:

- Learn about the other areas applicable to several of the courses our training team was designing.
- Enhance my resume with additional knowledge and experience.
- Position myself for a promotion.

I declined that job rotation because I was comfortable in my role at the time. Look back to situations where you failed to take advantage of an opportunity to learn or relearn. This is a part of our development path, because we don't just learn lessons from our own actions and mistakes but those of other people as well. However, we still need our adaptability to kick in as the backup to the backup. This prompts the need for development through the practice of planning your steps and learning from mistakes.

One example may go like this. A new system implementation is under way, and you are a part of the team designated to conduct the training on it. A new system update confused you in the course but you need things to go by the book. Although you may be tech savvy, you can enhance your skill by practicing learning agility. Learn all that you can in the amount of time you have prior to facilitating by practicing common tasks learners will perform in the system, accessing the help option, brainstorming questions learners may have, and collecting additional supplemental resources to put yourself in a better position to facilitate it. It makes a difference. I learned this from experience, having led a training course that could have been much better instead of only garnering average ratings and a series of questions I could not answer. How can we relate this to adaptability? I see a link in being willing to learn and relearn as needed.

For another example, let's say you have a group of learners that's different from the target audience the course was designed to address. You find out when you conduct the icebreaker and realize that a few of the exercises may not be appropriate. What do you do? Obtain learner feedback, identify their planned system usage, revise the objectives, and quickly adjust the learning activities. That is just something we do as facilitators, demonstrating high AQ to promote engaging learning experiences. If you are a facilitator or an instructor, how often do you customize learning activities in the course design, using creativity and innovation, to make them more engaging for your learners? My learners amazed me with their level of engagement the first time I did this. What else do you think would be applicable to adaptability in that example? See if you can recall a past experience where you can relate your mistake to a failure to learn or relearn.

Let's consider one more scenario. A client has requested an online storytelling course design for internal staff as a way to develop their consulting skills. You had on your consultant's hat and asked all of the right questions to create a blended learning experience as the instructional designer. After the first iteration, the client shares feedback that it does not seem modern and it feels too much like a clickable PowerPoint, with some animation and hot links. Now they also want to make it a package of short microlearning pieces instead of what was originally requested. You tell the client that it is too late to do anything significantly different in order to meet their deadline. With some critical thinking and problem solving, you might have been able to come up with a storytelling curriculum that could be designed with options such a podcast, short videos with whiteboard animation, an interactive infographic, an interactive PDF, an e-book, and quick knowledge check activities. Adapting to changes in requests or needs can be approached like solving a problem; you just need to apply some critical thinking, like in this instance. As you think about your approach to addressing this type of project change, apply your adaptability to work under pressure with critical thinking, creativity, taking risks, and communicating to the client.

Part of building an adaptive mindset is not just recognizing our mistakes but learning from our failures. In one of my previous job roles, I had to write blogs and social media posts. Our write-ups had to be reviewed and approved prior to being posted or published to our site. I had a few blows to my ego when I learned that the company did not like a couple of my submissions. But sometimes we have to brush off negative feelings and see the disguised opportunity for growth beneath the surface. Just don't take it personally.

I accepted the feedback and took my writing in another direction as suggested to better align it to the organization's preference, and my submissions were approved. I realized that there was a difference between what the organization was looking for to promote its brand, our services, and how we communicated it. There was the goal of letting workers know how the organization's brand should be promoted to their consultants because they had recently made some changes. Certain steps would be required of the consultants to stay in alignment with the brand while rendering services to external clients. Learning leaders within one of the teams viewed storytelling as a unique way to communicate the brand changes while demonstrating some of them in the process. This made sense to me, and did not deter me in my desire to render quality work.

Here is where some encounter a significant barrier, because they need to be perfect, or they need acceptance the first time, or they take rejection personally. These thoughts and mental responses impede development and positive performance. They can also crush adaptability efforts. I will not say that I have never been guilty of this; I have come to realize that I need to be conscious of my self-talk. There are times when your self-talk needs to be activated to tune out nonconstructive or negative external communications. This is simply noise that we must sometimes ignore. We can't ignore those occasions in which we need to change the channel for our self-talk because you are telling yourself things that do not contribute to an adaptive mindset.

And although the organization was not able to see the value in my original work, I thought my articles had potential. My determination to serve a purpose with what I thought was quality writing paid off for me with acceptance to ATD's *TD* magazine and *Training* magazine. These articles then landed me the opportunity for this book. At the end of the day, it is most important for you to see yourself as indispensable and put forth the effort to promote that perception to others.

 Consider This
- What are two mistakes you have made in a work role that taught you a lot?
- What is an example of a failure that helped lead you to a success at a later point?

Believe You Can Do It

What about those who feel like a fake or a substitute who was just lucky enough to land the opportunity? Someone with those thoughts and feelings may be experiencing impostor syndrome. It's not uncommon, but it can be detrimental to success because it diminishes the type of mindset and effort that go into growth and development. So another component to learning from failure and building your adaptive mindset is to ditch impostor syndrome.

In *The Art of War*, Sun Tzu states that you need to starve a well-fed enemy and force his movement when he's in a state of rest. Impostor syndrome is that enemy, and you have to stop feeding that attitude. This syndrome is a type of self-identity that limits one's potential. Think about it using the following example. When I took over coordinating a conference more than a decade ago, I noted the best practices of those before me and the lessons they learned. Despite this, my confidence level was not very high, and I had an episode of impostor syndrome regarding how well my first conference went. It was a major event with an anticipated audience of about 300, with a few breakout sessions. Internalizing successes is a major stumbling block for those with impostor syndrome. One literature review found that up to 82 percent of people experience impostor syndrome regardless of organizational level, profession, or industry (Bravata et al. 2020).

I've found that reflecting on past accomplishments is an effective way to combat impostor syndrome. Reflecting on the thoughts that were making me feel like an impostor is even more important—I have to remind myself that I must be my biggest champion rather than my strongest critic. I tell myself that my performance, my relationships, and my determination are creating these opportunities. How people combat impostor syndrome varies by each individual, but if it's something you experience, determine whether your approach is effective. If not, try something different to shift your mindset to acknowledging that the new responsibility is well deserved. Once I was able to overcome my impostor syndrome, I recognized the potential "to do me" and own my wins.

And lastly, what we learn from experience is not just for keeping to ourselves. Some people fail to share ideas that can result in improvements or new developments for the benefit of those in their circle, on their team, or within their close network. You can encourage others who may need that nudge to contribute their thoughts. I found myself in this situation with a co-worker who had a great idea that I had to persuade her to share. She was fearful of rejection and had previously encountered resistance to her ideas. These types of experiences are common, but they are examples of what is contrary to an adaptive mindset.

I am sure it's apparent to you that being a victim or a victor of change is a choice that's rooted in your mindset. Before you experience success, you must achieve it in your attitude and mindset. Otherwise, you have already failed. This is a point that can be easily missed. Unpredictable conditions reveal who we are and what we have the potential to be. Your mindset is your ignition key to drive improvement through setbacks. Keep a mindset that feeds your vision and not your fears. The extent to which you embrace an adaptive mindset depends on your perception of the need, and if you envision potential positive impact.

CHAPTER 7

Embrace Challenges

During the required residency for my doctoral study, I did a brief tour of Pearl Harbor in Hawaii, and it happened to coincide with the anniversary of the attack. During the attack, too many wounded were coming into the US Naval Hospital for them to handle. It was one of multiple facilities treating the wounded. A doctor told a nurse that they needed to start marking the foreheads of the wounded in order to indicate who had received medication. Once they could no longer use their felt markers, one nurse started using her lipstick to mark them. This was one small example of capacity for decisive action when forced to adapt. Someone's innovation skill became a part of history, and yours can too, as representative of your adaptability.

People with an adaptive mindset embrace challenges and view them as opportunities for improvement and innovation. This is a guiding factor in how you approach your ability to adapt and your opportunities for development. One way is to develop an adaptive mindset through challenges. If someone asked your peers or direct reports what they observe about you in response to challenges, think about how they would respond. Those challenges could be a difficult client, a process change, a rejected proposal, or a new role in the organization. Do you rise to challenges or run from them?

Why We Need to Embrace Challenges

In a constant countdown to the next change for learning and development, the need for adaptability in talent development roles remains the same. Our work must show adaptability in the midst of a crisis, an ongoing technology disruption, or an uncertain future. Are you leaving the best impression through your work? Think about the courses you design, tools you create, ideas you initiate, and projects you identify. Will your legacy be one of adaptability?

Whether you are an instructional designer, a trainer, a facilitator, a learning specialist, an HR specialist, a media developer, a project manager, or a learning leader, you may have the role of disruptor. This can be a good thing when your disruption leads to transformation for the better or some type of improvement. Disruptors question the norm, and they don't mind breaking things. We touched on this in chapter 3. The breaking comes by way of taking a risk with a design idea, venturing outside tradition, testing a theory with a programming method, or initiating a deviation from organizational norms. When you do what you have always done, you will get what you have always gotten.

Although it's not always the ideal situation, a crisis opens the door for talent development professionals to identify problems and determine plausible solutions. For growth and progress, we usually need a break in the normal course of doing what we have always done. That is certainly what we need in L&D, and you are responsible for making it happen.

Responding to Uncertainty

Responding to uncertainty often means getting out of your comfort zone. Well, for just about everyone, that's easier said than done. One reason is that people are usually ready to jump on the bandwagon rather than move forward alone. Going along with the crowd can impede the flow of disruptive ideas. Following along with what everyone else is saying or doing without question does not allow for a disruptive train of thought. This is where some fail to let their unique selves think and speak freely, while others choose to take the risk of the disruptive road less traveled. In the instances you find yourself working on something with a group, be conscious of whether you let your thoughts flow freely, or if you silence your inner self and only take in the thoughts of others, without contributing out of fear or insecurity. This is one major reason everyone does not excel with adaptability, because it also requires intentionality to truly bring your AQ game, as we learned early in the book.

Another reason for this is the fact that adaptability is expected, yet companies don't develop employees for adaptability. Business writing, customer service, diversity, EQ, leadership development, and time management are common training topics aligned to typical expectations in our work roles. Leaders should communicate expectations for worker adaptability and show action to support it. This action includes adding the topic to training curriculums, encouraging employees to think outside the box, and being open to ideas when they do.

A final reason that few get out of their comfort zone and enter the realm of adaptability is that they are not given the time to do so. It requires time to be creative, think of innovative ideas, and take a risk. Promoting adaptability has to be reflected as a regular part of your schedule as well as your individual attitude, mindset, behavior, and work performance.

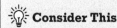 **Consider This**
- How do you embrace challenges?
- What are some examples you can identify for your adaptability track record?

Innovate and Disrupt

The compass, wheel, airplane, and telephone have a common denominator: They are inventions and technologies that transformed our lives. They are also inventions that have affected the way we work. There was a time in history when we had to depend on the sun and stars for our true north without any device. There was a time when we could not travel by air. Someone's persistence and drive pushed them to a level of innovation that revolutionized the way we travel and work today. And today's inventions are changing how we will work tomorrow. This provides us with subtle warnings to take steps today to prepare for change in the future of work.

How are you breaking away from old patterns and identifying new ways to accomplish a task or meet a goal? The face of learning is changing along with its approach. We see many organizations moving from pushing learning content to making learning available for learners to pull it as they need it when it is convenient for them, so it needs to be accessible. If you can avoid getting stuck in traditional practices and assist your organization in identifying approaches that meet learning requirements at the moment of need, you are exercising some adaptability. Look at the work tasks you complete and those of your team members. Re-examine them with a thought for the end in mind and a more efficient way to get there with a new strategy, software application, process, or redesigned plan.

Technology has become an essential factor that you can leverage for adaptability when you view it as something that can work for you rather than against you. Are you an individual who views technology as a friend or foe? If it's the latter, then you must change your perspective. Take a look at this as it relates to conducting training. We've discussed the mistake of trying to duplicate what you do in an in-person event for a virtual event. The same applies to transitioning to virtual work meetings, because each environment has its own advantages and disadvantages. We can expect to see ongoing development of features and tools to enhance the functionality for collaboration, notes capturing, and document sharing. This will require users to become comfortable and more efficient in the virtual meeting space.

The use of virtual platforms has replaced the boardroom. Enhanced features in e-learning tools such as Articulate Rise simplify the development step in instructional design with built-in programming. In the past, client organizations were looking for learning management systems to assign learning tracks based on competencies attached to roles. In the future, we could see solutions that can analyze employee behavior, work performance, and education data to create custom learning tracks based on capabilities for specific work or certain roles and provide coaching through a chat bot.

Other areas of talent development are evolving thanks to new technology. The training design space is experiencing an extreme overhaul in methodology when we look at the way virtual reality, augmented reality, and artificial intelligence are being leveraged. We are seeing more experiential learning with the inclusion of real-life situations and examples that allow learners to apply skills that duplicate what they may experience in a work situation. Learning metrics and analytics are also areas changing how we are advancing our efficiency with technology. Quicker access to training data and the analytics that reveal the patterns and meaning of the data leaves us without an excuse for making more informed decisions for improving talent development practices. An example of this would be using Power BI (business intelligence) to create a dashboard of learner course completion and learner online behavior to look at analytics or patterns and interpretations of the data rather than a simple PowerPoint pie chart of the raw data itself. This could guide decisions on redesigning training opportunities, discontinuing certain training, or enhancing your organization's training portfolio, because you are making evidence-based decisions, and technology equips you to do it quicker and easier. There is a significant difference between looking at a graph or chart and looking at several charts that you can manipulate as your leaders or team members ask questions about the data to gain a better understanding.

Rethink your perspective of technology in various areas, as you seek opportunities to leverage it with greater adaptability.

Workplace design has changed since employees returned to work and the process is ongoing for other organizations that are still designing for the future of work. Safety protocols including physical distancing are guiding factors as we navigate the new normal that continues to evolve. Talent agility has become imperative for organizations. This prompts the need for training, but training has to be approached differently, especially for in-person or hybrid workplaces. Additional technology has been added to many workplace environments to assist with worker safety, workplace learning, organizational communication, workplace change, and working differently in the new normal. With the return of workers to the physical workplace, reboarding has become popular because of the need to onboard returning employees who were working remotely. Employees are learning a new way of working, interacting with others, and handling the adjustment mentally and emotionally.

Communication tactics and tools are changing in response to the shifting workplaces and remote workers. Even organizations that were limited to email, newsletters, and an intranet had to diversify their tactics with technology advancements that promote communication up, down, and across. Those other options could include social media, blogs, press releases, online videos, and surveys. Slack, Google Hangouts, and Microsoft Teams are examples of apps that can bring workers and teams together while apart. These apps promote engagement with the use of collaboration features, such as real-time post capability and different channels for topics, file sharing, and messaging. I found myself researching collaboration tools and picking up recommendations during a few ATD chapter events. Organizations that are able to adjust and implement modernized alternatives reflect a higher AQ.

You can help build the organization's AQ as you work on building your own AQ. It can be mutually beneficial, and that is where I see how it is so important to you. Take advantage of the communication tactics and tools your organization makes available for you to collaborate with your colleagues, learn more about your business areas and functions, build your network within your organization, implement in training you conduct, use for sharing learning resources, and strengthen your interpersonal communication skills. All of these are ways for you to improve your adaptability.

DIAL: Diagnose, Imagine, Analyze, Leverage

An employee recognition program, a kickoff plan for a new system, and an employee engagement initiative with the community were more than what I expected my participants to create in my project management workshop for my master's degree. I designed it for my thesis and was able to add to the course offerings in my organization at the time. There was no project management basics training of any sort, and I saw my school project as an opportunity to kill two birds with one stone. Little did I know that this was an early sign of what would become a habitual response. How are you taking advantage of the doors that open for you to share an idea or contribute something you created or developed? Look for ways you can be the missing link with an idea for a new learning program, a process improvement, a new technology platform suggestion, or a better learning strategy. Think about what things are important to your organization. Consider the gap areas based on where your organization wants to be and where it is. Determine steps you can take to help get it there. You should record how you take advantage of these opportunities as well. These opportunities become your resume builders, cover letter highlights, and interview examples that present concrete evidence of your adaptability.

My need to add innovation and take the initiative reflected my adaptability. I realized that a few things were happening. I was turning my adaptability DIAL. Here is what I mean by that:

D I diagnosed a problem, gap, or opportunity for improvement.

I I imagined the future with a solution in place.

A I analyzed to determine what skills, resources, and time would be needed to fill the gap or make the improvement.

L I leveraged my skills, capabilities, and resources available to create a solution.

This was a dial that I intentionally turned to address new or changed conditions.

Let's look at each step in the DIAL process. The first step, problem diagnosis, focuses on what you are dealing with before you act. Are your efforts geared toward solving a problem, filling a gap because something is missing, or improving upon something that is already in place? The second step is taking time to create your vision of the ideal state, with the solution to the problem in place, the gap filled, or the process improvement implemented. The third step is your analysis of what you have at your disposal.

It is your review of skills you possess, capabilities in terms of what you have the ability to develop, and other resources, such as your network of relevant contacts. The fourth step is leveraging what you identified in the third step to achieve your goal. The more thorough your work in completion of the first three steps, the more likely you are to succeed in the final step. But practice is key, and you need to make the model work for your adaptability development purposes.

As you review the remainder of the chapter, think about a situation for applying this model. I would suggest applying the adaptability DIAL to a current or recent situation and complete each step to gain practice with it. You can complete the steps as an exercise (Figure 7-1). We may go through various process models for problem solving or program development, but I view this model as a way to relate those approaches to your personal development, not replace them. I see the adaptability DIAL as a wonderful tool for intentional development when you make it a part of your routine work behavior. Here is a breakdown:

- Diagnosing the situation at hand is the initial step to determine what needs to be done.
- Imagining the future allows us to discover and create, which leads to innovation. We see a glimpse of what could be.
- Analyzing means looking at what is available and accessible for use in solving the problem, filling the gap, or making the improvement.
- Leveraging is the final step in making it happen.

We can mistakenly overlook areas in our current roles where we are applying adaptability without realizing it. Take a moment to really think about it. Do you try to apply new things you have learned? Are you checking with contacts and networking to collaborate on ideas? What research steps do you take to learn a better approach to your problem or situation? Is it common for you to deviate from the norm? Answers to these questions establish your track record when it comes to your mode of response to a crisis, new conditions, or an unplanned change.

Figure 7-1. Adaptability DIAL Exercise

How can you turn your Adaptability DIAL and apply it to a work situation?

D Diagnose the problem, gap, or opportunity for improvement:

_____

I Imagine the future with a solution:

_____

A Analyze to determine what skills, resources, and time are needed:

_____

L Leverage skills, capabilities, and resources available:

_____

For the example, in my city role, I created a new multiday workshop that provided the fundamentals of project management by taking participants through the life cycle of a project they would have to complete from start to finish. I thought it would be a dual advantage to use the workshop for my master's project while adding it to the city's course offerings.

Use of the adaptability DIAL was the driver for me to ask our training manager to add my workshop. In this situation, there was a gap to be filled, since we did not have a similar program (the first step in DIAL). I had an instructor who inspired me and helped me recognize how although project management is a strong element in the foundation of many talent development initiatives, as it reaches across departments and work roles. I imagined how anyone working on a project could benefit from training on the basics to be more efficient in their project work, practice efficient project planning, and build confidence in their skills with better project outcomes (the second step in DIAL). I analyzed the skills I had attained from my degree program up to that point in course design, my capability to learn more, and resources available through my organization and school (the third step in DIAL). I leveraged skills gained in project management and other areas, as well as online, school, and work resources to complete my project thesis, which resulted in a project management program that was offered to thousands of workers (the fourth step in DIAL). Once the training was added to our program offerings, I had the momentum to do more in my role. This is something you are also able to achieve, and it need not have any relation to a school degree program.

Consider where your efforts can serve multiple purposes as you turn the DIAL. Contributing ideas within your organization is one purpose that can work in tangent with building your own adaptability. If you can address a gap or problem at the organizational level, what benefit could that bring to you and your organization as you pursue adaptability development? Not all organizations have a culture that promotes this type of initiative. There is a difference in the way you feel when taking the initiative is welcomed and successful, versus not being welcome. That difference influences future efforts in adaptability for many people, as shared in chapter 1. Your response can be a sign of whether your organization presents a culture of adaptability. However, the ultimate progress in your DIAL for adaptability development depends on you, not the organization's culture.

ADAPT-ing Your Training

Your training design should give employees what they crave—and what they don't. Not many of us can say that we always know what is best for our development without a little guidance and coaching. Employees may be in the same predicament. We can support leaders in their talent agility efforts to foster successful internal change within the workforce. Employees often focus their skill development on areas connected to tasks they must perform in a current role or on required skills for a promotional opportunity, with little to no attention on future-readiness skills. Those skills that we discussed in the first part of the book are the ones you will want to apply in your work, which increases your AQ. We can recap a few from our list: innovation, creativity, the ability to unlearn and relearn, flexibility, resilience, and problem solving. The adaptability we put into action is also the adaptability we want to develop in others.

I recommend the ADAPT approach as an early step in recognizing and addressing the need for adaptability:

- **Assess** your need for AQ development with a look at your response to adversity and how it is reflected in your productivity and performance. This is where you can determine your level of need for adaptability. It is an assessment of your AQ level.
- **Determine** what type of AQ skill development you need by targeting areas in assessment results. You must understand the types of situations, pressures, changes, and responsibilities you face when addressing your AQ. This will guide you in creating specific development goals. Your development goals should be based on where you are.
- **Analyze** the resources available internally and externally to complete your AQ development. A lot of training content is free and at almost anyone's disposal. Check what is available in massive open online courses (MOOCs), communities of practice, and other open source content. Coaching, mentoring, podcasts, TED Talks, job aids, and microlearning are other examples of resources that can be leveraged for development.
- **Prepare** a plan to achieve your goals and evaluate success. Take the results from the first three steps (assess, determine, and analyze) and pull your plan together. It should outline who, what, when, and how. This plan includes an evaluation element to measure results.
- **Take action** and seek training according to your plan for increasing your AQ. Various training options include e-learning, articles, podcasts, books, videos, blogs, and case studies.

You will find more information to assist you with your development approaches in chapter 8.

The type of content needed for developing adaptability depends on the skills targeted. Let's say that you have assessed the skills you need to develop, and have identified your development focus. If you need digital transformation, creativity, and learning agility, design training that promotes technology use, idea generation with collaboration, and the need to unlearn practices while relearning others. Being creative in your approach and the training you pursue by using technology positions you to achieve your adaptability objectives. Other options for development are reflection journals, accountability partners, situational exercises, and team collaboration activities. Remember the importance of building time into your schedule for creativity and idea generation as emphasized in an earlier chapter. I have found this step to beneficial to my time management. Keep the focus on the skills you are developing, and be open to situations that lend themselves to this, even when they are not planned.

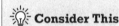 **Consider This**
- How can you benefit from routine use of the adaptability DIAL?
- What initial steps can you take to start applying the ADAPT model?

Take on Special Projects

Embracing challenges doesn't always mean disrupting what you already do. Special projects open another avenue for you to reveal your adaptive mindset. Let's say a special projects team or task force is started and you have the opportunity to join. This holds potential for you to apply your strengths, gain experience, develop skills you may lack, and make a contribution you can add to your resume.

In talent development or any profession, a mind is a terrible thing to waste on anything that does not promote your growth and development for greater adaptability. An adaptive mindset will equip you for development and growth. What is a recent experience where you applied an adaptive mindset, or needed to if you did not? How could you envision that experience having a different result with your adaptive mindset?

In a 1994 interview, Steve Jobs explained that once you realize that you have the mental capacity to change the world around you, it will change you forever. Some are fearful of this without even realizing it; often, it is the fear that they will actually be successful. That's real talk for your road to development. If you think you can change the world, you can become one of the ones who do.

As I reflect on some past experiences, a few stand out as examples of my adaptability track record. One year my department instituted task force committees for different organizational initiatives. I ended up in a committee handling employee engagement. We were a team that knew one another but did not work together. We were given only a vague description of what the committee was commissioned to do. My enthusiasm and passion for the work made me a good fit to take the lead in our committee, developing a 12-month strategic plan that was not even requested. It included surveys for feedback, a charitable marathon, a bowling outing, focus groups, a back-to-school supplies drive where employees would donate supplies and make a sundae of their choice (Back-to-School Treats and Eats), learning-based gamification activities, and other efforts. I was enjoying the work that required me to stretch, and I could identify ways that my background and skill could fill a gap and provide an improvement.

How often do you question yourself about taking on duties outside your job description or assignments? This is certainly appropriate, but you should consider a few things in answering that question. For me, the answer is not always the same for every situation; it depends on the end goal, the return on investment (both short term and long term), and resources needed such as the amount of time I must allocate. This was a part of my thought process and a way of applying an adaptive mindset. Practice thinking about how you can contribute even on a small scale if you don't have sufficient time to dedicate to a project or task. Our employee engagement collaboration generated innovative approaches that started with my idea of us taking the committee further. We achieved such a high degree of success with our creative approaches that we became the go-to committee for special projects that should have been assigned to other divisions or committees. We had established a brand for our committee in the department—we were the "HR One Team" and we were proud of it, because we were about serving the department staff at every level. Employee morale reached a point where employees were coming to us with unsolicited ideas for events outside the office, community engagement, process improvement, and technological advancement.

In another role, I was assigned to lead our training team in creating an HR University curriculum with 15 modules. Sure, I had designed previous courses from scratch, but this was different. I was leading the team in the design and development of 15 modules, with facilitator guides, PowerPoint presentations, participant manuals, and additional materials, all of which needed to be completed within a few months. A combination of fear and excitement consumed me as I went to work on it with the team. I collaborated with the team on a different strategy and layout from that of other materials we developed in-house. We established a vision for the project that was aligned to the HR director's vision for the effort. In adapting myself to the role, I thought about great examples I saw modeled. I reflected on the skills I covered in courses I facilitated, and I considered the people on my team as well as what I learned about them from working together. These were key areas in helping me face challenges with different work styles and opinions, and in addressing accountability when something was not completed.

Rising to the Challenge

We have to do things in an unconventional manner. You won't discover your adaptability potential until you face a situation that requires you to step out of your comfort zone. But we all have adaptability potential to unleash, so stop viewing your ability as a weakness and determine how it may actually be your superpower.

Think about taking a risk in terms of this analogy. I am not a basketball player, but I am a fan when it's time for the playoffs. I was having a conversation with a friend about a chance she took in making a suggestion to their director. They explained that they had no qualms about it. It was like a player who doesn't mind going for that three-point shot, versus the player who passes it up because they might miss. The one who takes the chance and goes for the shot knows that another opportunity is coming later, because the game isn't over. The other player decides not to take it because it will ruin their shooting percentage. Which one is the high-AQ player, and which one are you? Just remember that you will have another opportunity to make the shot. The journey you help someone else take through the door of adaptability comes after you have gone through your own, so you are able to lead the way.

CHAPTER 8
Adapt Your Career

If the World Economic Forum had predicted in 2018 that we could see as many as 75 million jobs disappear by 2022, then we'd need to give thought to potential jobs coming onto the scene and what they would mean for being adaptable in your career. But note that the disappearance of jobs should not be confused with the elimination of work; the people who held those lost jobs will go to other roles or functions. At the executive level, we have seen strategy, diversity, technology, and engagement become essential. Already some organizations have a chief amazement officer, chief culture officer, chief data officer, chief digital officer, chief engagement officer, chief experience officer, or a chief happiness officer, like at McDonald's.

In 2010, Dell and Kodak introduced their chief listening officers (Slutsky 2010). These roles handle social media intelligence gathering and community management to learn what is said about the organization and to help it become more strategic in internal and external communication. Dell had acquired Perot Systems in 2009, making long-term efforts for growth and efficiency as it expanded into IT solutions for customers. Kodak was not quick enough to establish its place in the realm of digital photography, and suffered its biggest financial loss as a result in 2009. As a result of these disruptions, both organizations had great need for a turnaround, and both experienced significant market response.

New executive-level roles are indicators of high-AQ organizations designating people to lead adaptability in organizational culture, digitization, engagement, and morale. Kodak and Dell are just two of the examples that have surfaced within the last decade. And since there is a chief for everything else, we could soon see chief adaptability officer in the C-suite.

And the executive level is not the only level responding to change with emerging job roles. Efforts to enable learning, drive collaboration, and maintain engagement remain important as ever. Roles such as learning experience (LX) designer, global creative visualization designer, digital coaching experience manager, and VR experience creator are growing more popular. Emergence of new talent development roles is not something you have to wait to see happen. You can proactively create one that connects your skill and passion to an organization's need.

Writing this chapter filled me with ideas to put on paper and see how emerging jobs and career expansion opportunities align to my personal goals. Where do you see adaptability potential in your work role or your career? Now is a good time to think about where you are in your career compared with where you aspire to be. The gap between the two is your free space to apply your adaptability skills toward your development and to level up to reach your goals. This chapter will offer you several tools to help you put this into practice.

Level Up Your Practice

"Level Up" is not only a song popularized by Ciara in 2018; the term also applies to navigating your career development. The first time I heard the song, I was in the roller skating rink with my nephews in 2019. I liked the beat, but I had to ask them what the singer was saying. The lyrics talk about moving on beyond our mistakes, learning from them, turning them into something, and coming back with continued elevation. If that doesn't sound like adaptability, I'm not sure what to tell you. I was sold and it was apparent how others were as well. From what I recall, the song took off beyond the entertainment industry. It popularized the phrase "level up" in workplace initiatives, conference themes, and various other places. Your readiness to level up your adaptability is about you progressing to the next level.

One way you can level up is with an adaptability LUPE, or "level up to progress on essentials." The level up is your work to bring your skills up to align with a standard, such as the Talent Development Capability Model. You may identify others, but this covers many of the essentials for talent development roles. Apply this strategy to your development for your adaptability skills.

 Consider This
- What are two to five goals for developing my adaptability?
- Where can I apply an adaptive mindset in my role?

Countless situations we encounter in workplace learning can present untapped opportunities to level up the "adaptable you." Do you recognize them when you encounter them? Table 8-1 lists examples of situations and how to respond on your road to adaptability. The first column explores potential situation types in the areas of progress essentials for adaptability. The second column discusses actionable steps where you can level up on these essentials. These steps are simply a few examples of the numerous ways to respond in order to strengthen your adaptability.

Table 8-1. Your Adaptability Level Up for Progress Essentials (LUPE)

Situations for Adaptability (Progress Essentials)	Response Example (Ways to Level Up on the Essentials)
New Environment	• Step outside your comfort zone and be willing to gain experience and form new relationships. • Exhibit a flexible attitude and a welcoming approach.
New Method	• Ask for guidance and help to understand changes. • Change your perception of the situation to recognize the potential for achieve the desired future state.
New Practices and Processes	• Seek clarification from team members and managers to help you plan for the transition. • Keep an open mind to learn new ways of doing things. • Encourage others to embrace change for improvement.

Table 8-1. Continued

Situations for Adaptability (Progress Essentials)	Response Example (Ways to Level Up on the Essentials)
New Situation	• Be open to learning from new people and experiencing new challenges for development. • Analyze your mindset and how others perceive you.
New Technology	• Demonstrate your learning agility and be ready to learn new technology with workplace advancements. • Research resources available in your workplace, online, and through formal training.
New Work Team	• Build new relationships and be open to sharing knowledge with others while learning from them as well. • Take the opportunity to learn about your ways of interacting with different work styles.
Changing Client and Customer Needs	• Ask questions to identify your understanding of needs. • Be an active listener via phone, online, or virtual communication. • Be concerned and interested in the client goals to assist in identifying needs. • Work on your emotional intelligence and show empathy.
Changing Internal and External Partnering	• Embrace the opportunity to grow in partnership experiences and form new relationships. • Look for ways to promote mutual benefits.
Changing L&D Ecosystem	• Practice learning agility. • Experiment with the latest tools and techniques. • Research options that fit your role, team, and organization. • Allow yourself to make mistakes.

Your development areas for adaptability can extend across a broad range. These are some of the common examples, and I am sure that you can identify many more after what has been covered on ways to build your AQ.

Set Your SMART Goals and Put Them in Writing

At this point, you are ready to start your LUPE, but where do you begin? You begin with the end in mind: your goal for your education, your development, your career, your adaptability, and anything else you set out to accomplish. When that vision is not clear or identified for yourself, you have a problem connecting the dots and making the right decisions. Failure to identify a goal inhibits you from creating a path to the goal. How can you tell if you are on the right path when you did not identify a goal before blazing a trail to it? Goals may be identified based on needs assessment results, being aware of your actual skill gaps, new work demands, technology changes, feedback, or your own desires and aspirations.

Once you've identified your goals, your work is not done. It's also a best practice to put your goals in writing. A 2015 study by Gail Matthews with the Dominican University of California found that individuals were more than 40 percent likely to achieve their goals when they made it a regular practice to write them down. I became accustomed to putting my goals in writing when I was certified as a First Things First instructor. It wasn't until I attended my first When Women Lead conference several years ago that I experienced a different type of appreciation for written goals, especially the ones I achieve. During the end of the speaker's presentation, she asked the audience to use the 3x5 index card she provided us to write down three goals we planned to achieve and the dates for them within the next few months. She said she would mail them to us as a follow-up and reminder of our commitment to ourselves. The presenter followed through as she said she would, and I received my card in the mail as promised. I remember how good it felt to receive my card and see that I had completed two goals I wrote down, and was due to completed the third shortly. That was such a small effort with mountainous impact for me. I encourage you to write down your adaptability goals. Someone said that until you write it down, it is only a dream. It's time to make some of your dreams become your reality.

It's a good practice to be SMART about your goal setting:

- **Specific:** answers the five Ws, *who, what, why, where,* and *which*
- **Measurable:** provides a quantitative element to track your progress
- **Achievable:** is challenging but reasonable to achieve
- **Relevant:** answers why it is important to you
- **Time-oriented:** gives a deadline for achieving the goal.

SMART goal setting is an effective practice for setting any goals you endeavor to achieve, not just development ones. Table 8-2 shows an adaptability development plan with two goal examples. You need this level of detail to execute a thorough plan that guides you through what you are doing, what is needed and when, and how you will know whether you are successful. Once you complete the goal, you can enter the "Actual Completion Date" for your records. Look online for templates to capture the same information in other layouts.

You can use the blank Adaptability Development Plan in the appendix to fill in your own goals, skills, activities, resources, dates, and success criteria.

 Consider This

- What are my three greatest areas of opportunity for developing my adaptability skills?
- What tools can I apply in the next 14 days? In the next 30 days?

Career Landscape Tool

In identifying my adaptability focus for a presentation in October 2020, I thought the "level up" theme would work perfectly for me. I was invited to speak when I had a host of other obligations, but I thought it would be a beneficial opportunity in promoting adaptability by contributing to an event that had helped me in the past, and the person asking just happened to be one of my mentors. I surely could not say no to Lee Meadows, president of the National Association of African Americans in Human Resources—State of Michigan (NAAAHR). I titled my presentation "Level

Table 8-2. Sample Adaptability Development Plan

Adaptability Development Goal	Skill or Capability	Resources	Methods and Activities	Target Date	Completion Date	Success Criteria
Create an e-learning course using Articulate Storyline 360 in the next 30 days	Technology or authoring tool	• Webinar • YouTube video • Job aid • vILT • E-learning industry articles and blogs	• Laptop • Internet access • Articulate Storyline 360 application	January 2023		• E-learning course with four objectives • A post-assessment • At least three learner interactions
Share at least two new innovative ideas with your work team or supervisor in the next 90 days	Innovation	• LinkedIn Learning webinar • *Chief Learning Officer* magazine • TED Talk • *Wired* magazine • Online courses	• ATD Chapter Special Interest Group (SIG)	March 2023		• Idea submitted to your supervisor, department head, or another leader

Up Your Adaptability 'Q' for Leadership 2020" for the When Women Lead annual conference with NAAAHR. Prior to this, I had done several presentations and a few podcasts during the pandemic shutdown period. It made sense because individuals, teams, and organizations were hungry for adaptability and best practices for its application.

As we navigate our careers, knowing how to recognize obvious and hidden opportunities is key. The conference invite was an easy choice to make. Some opportunities are similarly apparent, while some require you to think beyond the surface level and consider long-term impact, such as purpose fulfillment, relationship building, network enhancement, development, name association, and paying it forward. These are just a few examples of factors I use to weigh the decisions that guide what can affect my career journey in the short term and the long term. Not everything will render an immediate return on investment.

During the Q&A, one attendee asked me about what they could tell a person who is not sure of what to do during the pandemic. I thought this was a great question and was excited to answer it, because it was a question I'd been answering for myself for the last two years, but more frequently in 2020. Our future's uncertainty leaves us in a state of little to no predictability, even about the career landscape in talent development. Rapid changes accompanied by emerging industries are reflections of the disruption occurring and the evolution of new careers. Instead of a growing concern about your employability, you can direct that energy toward making your AQ soar. Embrace uncertainty as you apply the tools and resources to create your desired outcomes for your career and development.

What's here today will look quite different tomorrow because industry changes lead to changes in our needs. We may see the need for learning experience designers who are able to design VR or AI training for soft skills and other topics not previously required, and storyboard them. VR and AI consultants might be additional positions that are developed. LinkedIn (2020) reports that 41 percent of L&D professionals feel that we could see more accurate personalization of content by leveraging AI. While we don't have a crystal ball to show us new careers, we are getting glimpses of where we're headed. For example, we see growing application of VR and AI to create learner experiences. Unlike humans, machines work 24/7/365, without the need for time off. A study by the Brandon Hall Group described how an application review workflow that takes a person one hour can be reduced to five minutes using machine learning. The workflow for enrolling someone in training and sending them a welcome letter can take a person 30 minutes; however, when using machine learning, that task can be completed in two minutes. Machine learning is a type of artificial intelligence that enables computers to act based on data and patterns without being programmed to do so. We are just beginning to harness greater levels of untapped potential with AI as we observe its widespread application across industries not limited to talent development.

There are some key talent development areas where we may see more machine learning. Talent acquisition, career planning, L&D, performance, engagement, and employee recognition could easily benefit from AI or machine learning, when applied to simple tasks that do not require a human touch. Some examples of tasks that we already see completed with AI are:

- Applicant processing
- Resume screening
- New hire processing
- Onboarding
- Matching competencies to work roles
- High potential leader tracking
- Learner course progress and completion
- Coaching for leadership development
- Employee benefits servicing
- Employee engagement channels
- Performance reviews
- Employee recognition programs

These are worth recognizing because they present areas in which we can concentrate on developing innovation, flexibility, creativity, problem

Table 8-3. Talent Development Career Landscape

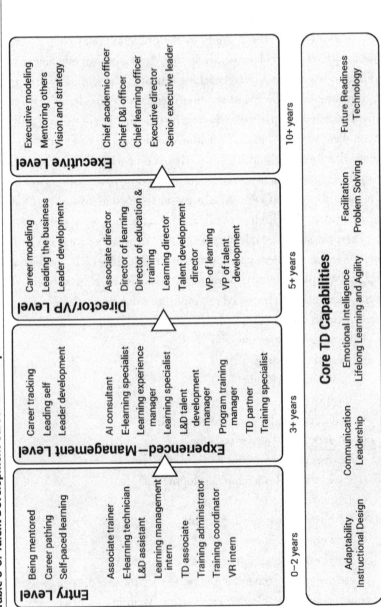

Entry Level
0–2 years

Being mentored
Career pathing
Self-paced learning

Associate trainer
E-learning technician
L&D assistant
Learning management intern
TD associate
Training administrator
Training coordinator
VR intern

Experienced—Management Level
3+ years

Career tracking
Leading self
Leader development

AI consultant
E-learning specialist
Learning experience manager
Learning specialist
L&D talent development manager
Program training manager
TD partner
Training specialist

Director/VP Level
5+ years

Career modeling
Leading the business
Leader development

Associate director
Director of learning
Director of education & training
Learning director
Talent development director
VP of learning
VP of talent development

Executive Level
10+ years

Executive modeling
Mentoring others
Vision and strategy

Chief academic officer
Chief D&I officer
Chief learning officer
Executive director
Senior executive leader

Core TD Capabilities

Adaptability
Instructional Design

Communication
Leadership

Emotional Intelligence
Lifelong Learning and Agility

Facilitation
Problem Solving

Future Readiness
Technology

solving, and critical-thinking skills with a future focus. We need one eye on what's happening today and another looking ahead to tomorrow. That alone requires practice, because it is a type of challenge that requires you to have your mind in two places at once.

As you think about where your career may take you, whether through promotions or skill development, consult this Career Landscape tool (Table 8-3). Fill out the template in the appendix with where you are and what skills you'll need to achieve your desired goal.

In this tool, review the titles that are characteristic of the levels displayed. Where you do you fit in? Core talent development capabilities are indicated as the foundation for all levels of your career journey. How do you match up? In each job level, you apply your adaptability skills as you continue developing the ones that represent your areas of opportunity. Some are more applicable to certain levels, such as promoting a high-AQ culture at the upper-management level. When completing your own landscape tool in the appendix, you should identify your current job role at the applicable level in your organization. What could this look like for you and other talent development professionals? Do your career planning efforts reflect your passions? Are you seeking the most desirable opportunities? Do you want to start your own consulting business?

Adaptability Cheat Sheet

One of my first presentations on adaptability included a cheat sheet. I called it that because it functioned as a quick and dirty resource for learning professionals and others. When you're ready for your adaptability development, there are some steps that can help you, shown in Table 8-4. I captured practical steps to take you through a process for your ongoing progression to a high AQ.

Each step has a brief description and indicates if you need to involve others in your completion of the step. For example, you can use feedback from others, as discussed in the Johari window, for your self-awareness. AQ-boosting skills, such as collaboration, learning from others, and innovation are additional examples with others involved rather than you acting solo. Put this cheat sheet into action with any necessary customizations to implement for your work role.

Table 8-4. Adaptability Cheat Sheet for Development

Step	Description	Involves Others
1. Apply an AQ model	Use a model, such as one covered in this book, as a way to focus your development.	
2. Take your AQ pulse	Reflect on your behaviors, skills, and past actions to determine where you are. See the appendix for more resources on formal adaptability assessments.	✓
3. Apply a development plan	Use your adaptability LUPE along with another tool to track your progress on specific goals you will set.	
4. Set your AQ goals and identify milestones	Set goals for yourself that you have identified with the power to pivot. Include stretch goals that promote your personal and professional growth.	
5. Identify challenges	Think about what obstacles will need to be addressed on the way to goal achievement.	
6. Research resources available	Look at requirements for your success in goal achievement. Resources can include webinars, online courses, workshops, TED Talks, podcasts, mentors, accountability partners, tutorials, professional association chapter meetings, special interest groups, book clubs, volunteer opportunities for leadership, work projects, committee work, and formal education.	✓
7. Practice steps to boost your AQ	Practice things such as flexibility, innovation, and learning agility. Review the adaptability LUPE and additional resources in the appendix.	✓
8. Sharpen your adaptability saw	Reflect on your achievements and instances where you were really in your adaptability zone and thrived. Share your progress with others, such as an accountability partner.	✓

Putting Adaptability to Work

Tools are only as good as their application. You need the right tools for the right job at the right time. I've shared a few tools throughout this book so you can use them to focus on skill development. These methods and models assist in your development because you can apply them as you gain experience in the field. These also work as springboards for you to put into practice what has been shared in the book. Consider how you can be creative, innovative, versatile, and flexible with the tools within your role. Look for ways that you can make something work better for you and your team. Your only limitation is you—your attitude and mindset.

CHAPTER 9

Hold Yourself Accountable

When it comes to accountability, I'll always recall my trip as a chaperone to teen students to Toyota City, Japan, in 2013. Over the course of a few weeks prior to leaving, we completed cultural training classes to assist us in preparing for the trip. These classes included guidelines, such as: Whatever you do, don't lose your passport! This was drilled into us as chaperones, along with the students. Of course, what happened the first day? One of the students misplaced her passport.

As we visited several places to narrow down where it could have been lost, I thought we were in a nightmare or a horrible episode of the Ashton Kutcher show *Punk'd!* The other chaperone and I eventually split up, with the students and our interpreters to assist us. All I could think about was, what in the world were we going to do if we did not find her passport? She needed it to return home: What do you say to a parent if they place their teenager in your hands to go to another country and you return without them?

Maybe an hour or so later, we returned to a location we'd searched and learned that someone had turned in the passport. It was a powerful accountability lesson for the students as well as for us chaperones. Taking responsibility for your actions is vital when you consider the decision making, critical thinking, risk taking, and related adaptability skills. Without accountability, the behaviors of a high-AQ individual can be damaging rather than a positive addition to a team.

Adaptability Stakes

In demonstrating adaptability, the stakes are always high when it comes to what is in your best interest professionally and personally. Does reading or hearing the word *accountability* cause you to cringe? Is it that go-to problem solver that organizations use to answer performance and results issues in the workplace? Before we learn the word, we are taught accountability. As children, we learn voluntarily or involuntarily that our actions and our lack of action have consequences, and that it is up to us to own them. I like the definition shared in *The Oz Principle*, by Roger Connors, Tom Smith, and Craig Hickman (2010): Accountability is "a personal choice to rise above one's circumstances and demonstrate ownership necessary for achieving desired results—to see it, own it, solve it, and do it."

Accountability is about what we do and don't do, and accepting responsibility for both. I relish using the following statement when I am nearing completion of a course I am teaching or facilitating: "You have obtained some tools and learned some skills to make you armed and dangerous." I believe that this should be a goal with almost anything we put our minds to do. We should be ready to become armed and dangerous to do the things that make a difference, are impactful, and help us to leave a legacy. This book was intended to set you on a path to do that, or to inspire you to continue on your high-AQ path, with the ultimate responsibility placed in your lap to make it happen.

"What else can I do to rise above my circumstances and get the results I want?" This is a question posed by *The Oz Principle* authors because your answer is the line that separates accountability from victimization. It's similar to the thin line between love and hate. However, you either choose to be a victim of circumstances or you don't. You accept what's within your control or you don't. I realized that this was a question that I asked myself regularly before reading that book. A few situations in my past have left me on the brink of feeling like I had no control and was powerless. These were the ones I shared earlier in the book. I found myself recognizing thoughts and mindsets that I needed to change. I did this by consulting go-to reads (favorite books like the Bible and *The 7 Habits of Highly Successful People*), reflecting on my achievements, and tapping into my support system, which are all areas for emphasis in this final chapter to wrap up your journey to adaptability.

Owning Your Adaptability Journey

Part of your initial approach is in recognizing your mindset and attitude in relation to your productivity and performance. Question yourself and your results. There's no usefulness in exerting mental energy on the blame game. You cannot control the other players, and most of the time there is no referee. It's about what you will do when you have control of the ball.

I have someone in my support system, Eileen, whom I tease about being my personal drill sergeant because of her standards and high expectations. Eileen demonstrates the type of iron that sharpens my iron. When I am holding myself accountable, I may ask myself, "What would Eileen tell me?" I know her well enough to answer, and it provokes me to stretch where I deem necessary, as well as to reflect on the points where I did not bring "high-potential Esther" to the game. It doesn't make a difference if you have strong game if you don't bring it.

Questioning your performance and productivity works in conjunction with your use of tools that help you achieve adaptability success. You received quite a few tools to add to your tool chest in chapter 7. The Career Adaptability Checklist, shown in Table 9-1, can aid you in holding yourself accountable. In addition, this tool provides a way to connect the other tools. Make the tool work for you with any necessary customizations to ensure regular application.

Table 9-1. TD Career Adaptability Checklist

Name: _____

This Career Adaptability Checklist is a tool for you or a person you are mentoring. Use this checklist to assist you (or your mentee) in recognizing opportunities to apply adaptability skills on the path to a high AQ. Essential steps are included to remind you about things that may be helpful as you navigate your career landscape. You are able to include additional steps you may identify for yourself along the way. Return to this checklist monthly or quarterly as you see fit. Choose the steps you plan to complete.

❑ Review adaptability methods and processes provided in *Adaptability in Talent Development*: Which methods or processes will I use? How and when?

_____

_____

❑ Complete Adaptability Assessment

❑ Complete a Personal Adaptability Skills Inventory (list those things that make you adaptable)

❑ Set adaptability SMART goals

❑ Start the TD Career Landscape

❑ Select tracking tool (journal or other) to capture daily or weekly application of adaptability skills: collaboration, creativity, curiosity, flexibility, innovation, optimism, risk taking, versatility, others:

_____

_____

❑ Evaluate your support system. Add or remove people as needed by identifying who helps fuel growth.

❑ Determine a planned approach to encouraging, motivating, or supporting others daily, weekly, or on another schedule, and add this to your development plan as a SMART goal.

Table 9-1. Continued

☐	Identify ways to stay updated on best practices, buzz topics, innovation, and trends in your field (articles, blogs, books, LinkedIn, and others). Add this to your development plan as a SMART goal.
☐	Identify barriers or challenges to your adaptability at work, home, or both: _____ _____
☐	Determine options to overcome barriers or challenges: _____ _____
☐	Choose frequency to track and evaluate development plan (weekly, monthly, or quarterly).

Other: _____

_____

_____

Other: _____

_____

_____

Your tools help you monitor and track your progress on your journey. Because this needs to work for you, you must give yourself the flexibility and liberty to make changes in the process. The changes may result from you changing your path, a change in your goals, a crisis, an unexpected event, or something else. Every tool and plan you use simply needs to align to your goals and keep you on track. You are a valuable commodity who continues to appreciate in value with your ongoing development using these essential tools.

Who Are Your Best Accountability Partners?

Who's in your corner? It's not just about what you know, but who you know when it comes to your development. The right people in your corner can make a world of difference. This was the case in *Million Dollar Baby*, with Hilary Swank and Clint Eastwood. Eastwood played a reluctant boxing trainer who gave Swank the guidance, coaching, feedback, recognition, and assistance she needed to become a champion and achieve goals beyond her expectations. Unfortunately, she forgot one important lesson that he taught her in a life-changing moment: Never turn your back on your enemy. When she did, her enemy gave her a blow that changed her life at the highest cost. The right people ringside can be your support system, but it is up to you to do the work, because you have the ultimate accountability.

 Consider This
- How can an accountability partner assist you on your journey?
- Where do you have accountability challenges?
- Who are examples of two potential accountability partners?

Often, your accountability partners have been where you are going or have experience that allows them to impart wisdom to assist you on your journey. They also tell you what you need to hear when you need to hear it, whether you want to or not. That is determined by the type of relationship you have built, and how safe you have made it for them to challenge you. Your accountability partners may be selected for the position or inadvertently end up in the position. It may be for a season or a given time period. The important point is that they hold you accountable beyond what you do for yourself. They may push the mark in a way that you would not or have not. They do not envy you, use you, abuse you, or ignore you. They do not say or do things that tear you down. The negative opinion of another should never become your reality. If your accountability partner does any of the negative things referenced, you may need to reevaluate the relationship.

I learned the practice of promoting accountability partners from another facilitator in a course I attended. You should realize by now that I am a big fan of what I see that works for someone else and implementing it in a way that works for me. If this is something you do as well, you are practicing adaptability. This is one of the many ways I have benefited from a good support system.

Selecting your best accountability partner should not be viewed as a trivial task or something you do without sincere thought. Ask yourself who comes to mind when you need someone to give you honest feedback about your work, your behavior, or your communication. You may even need more than one person. Keep this in mind as you review the following tips assist you in your selection:

- Choose a peer.
- Choose someone trustworthy.
- Choose someone who challenges you, and doesn't criticize you.
- Choose someone who has your best interest at heart.
- Choose someone who will be assertive and have the courage to tell you when you are falling short.

The work with your best accountability partner should focus on the adaptability goals you have set and the progress to achievement, along with discussions of challenges and barriers. Those whom I pull from my support system to be my best accountability partners are essential to my success for certain goals in achieving a high AQ. For example, I share my goals with Laura and Eileen, and they know enough about me to provide useful feedback. It is up to you how much you choose to enlarge the arena or open area of your Johari window. Your partner's insights can go only as deep as the foundation of information they have.

You may not need them to do a deep dive with you. You can have a surface-level accountability partner who is there to exchange updates and feedback on your progress to goal achievement and nothing more.

However, I would suggest maintaining records of your follow-up with your accountability partner. Doing this routinely helps me to take notes on my progress and discussion items, but it doesn't have to be anything formal. Make it work for your purposes.

The Measure-Up

The time is coming for you to reflect on what you set out to do, what you did, how well you did it, and the reason why. Most important here is the why, as advocated by Simon Sinek in his book *Start With Why* (2009). This will help you understand the reason for doing something before getting into the how. I find more meaning and value in my results and goal achievement with my why identified. It's like how I initially pursued a doctorate—I was often told by family and friends that they expected me to pursue a doctorate, so I did. However, I didn't start with my why. Later, when courses became harder, the work grew more grueling, and I felt like throwing in the towel, I learned the importance of having a true why to keep myself going. Once I established that, I was able to recommit to achieving my goals. Your measure is your view of your goal achievement and the work you did to see it, own it, solve it, and do it.

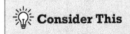 **Consider This**

How will you record and track the actions you want to take for your development?

We have come to the end of our journey, and the power lies with you to make some decisions. This is the start of the next phase, with you applying what you have learned and sharing it. The Roman philosopher Seneca said, "When we teach, we learn." You are ready to place some demands on your own potential, and everything laid out in the nine chapters of this book has shown you how. You learned about what adaptability is, the need for it, and the benefits to you in part 1. In part 2, you learned some steps to put adaptability into practice for various talent development roles, with tools to assist you in the process.

Let me leave you with some inspiration I heard in a speech by author, speaker, leadership consultant, and minister Myles Munroe. He shared an analogy of how eagles respond to storms:

- The eagle looks for storms and doesn't fear them.
- The eagle uses the storm to choose the height it needs to reach to the rise above it.
- The eagle uses the storm to rest. It knows the storm is temporary.
- The eagle uses a storm to cleanse its feathers and to test itself.
- The eagle lets storms leave when they're done.

You can approach your storm, crisis, or situation of unexpected change like an eagle and allow it to bring forth your adaptability with a high AQ. It's not until we stretch ourselves and excel to new heights that we grow. During the next storm that comes your way, remind yourself that you were built for this. The next time you take a look in the mirror, you should be looking for your new face of adaptability outside your comfort zone: the more adaptable you, personally and professionally, with the potential to become the soaring eagle you were meant to be, if you have not already. I see great things to come for you, and this will be your AQ game changer.

Appendix

Talent Development Capability Model

Leverage the Talent Development Capability Model to guide your skill building with consideration of future readiness and meeting organizational needs.

Adaptability Cheat Sheet for Development

Step	Description	Involves Others
1. Apply an AQ model	Use a model, such as one covered in this book, as a way to focus your development.	
2. Take your AQ pulse	Reflect on your behaviors, skills, and past actions to determine where you are. See the appendix for more resources on formal adaptability assessments.	✓
3. Apply a development plan	Use your adaptability LUPE along with another tool to track your progress on specific goals you will set.	
4. Set your AQ goals and identify milestones	Set goals for yourself that you have identified with the power to pivot. Include stretch goals that promote your personal and professional growth.	
5. Identify challenges	Think about what obstacles will need to be addressed on the way to goal achievement.	
6. Research resources available	Look at requirements for your success in goal achievement. Resources can include webinars, online courses, workshops, TED Talks, podcasts, mentors, accountability partners, tutorials, professional association chapter meetings, special interest groups, book clubs, volunteer opportunities for leadership, work projects, committee work, and formal education.	✓
7. Practice steps to boost your AQ	Practice things such as flexibility, innovation, and learning agility. Review the adaptability LUPE and additional resources in the appendix.	✓
8. Sharpen your adaptability saw	Reflect on your achievements and instances where you were really in your adaptability zone and thrived. Share your progress with others, such as an accountability partner.	✓

ADAPT Model

Implement the ADAPT model on your journey to increase your AQ.

ADAPT Model

Analyze
Analyze the resources available internally and externally to complete your AQ development.

Determine
Determine what type of AQ skill development is needed by targeting your areas from assessment results.

Prepare
Prepare a plan to achieve your goals and evaluate success.

Assess
Assess the need for your AQ development with a look at your response to adversity and how it is reflected in your productivity and performance.

Take Action
Take action and take training according to your plan for increasing your AQ.

The FAST Approach

Apply the FAST approach to create a culture of adaptability in your organization.

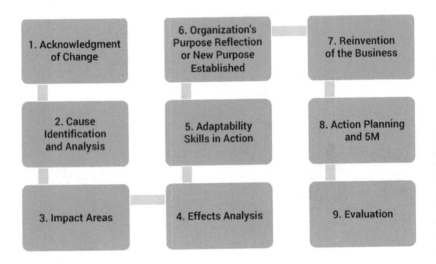

Adaptability Development Plan

Use this Adaptability Development Plan to track and monitor your progress in pursuing your adaptability goals.

Adaptability Development Goal	Skill or Capability	Resources	Methods and Activities	Target Date	Completion Date	Success Criteria

TD Career Landscape and Template

Apply the Talent Development Career Landscape and Template in setting goals to map your career as a talent development professional with upward mobility.

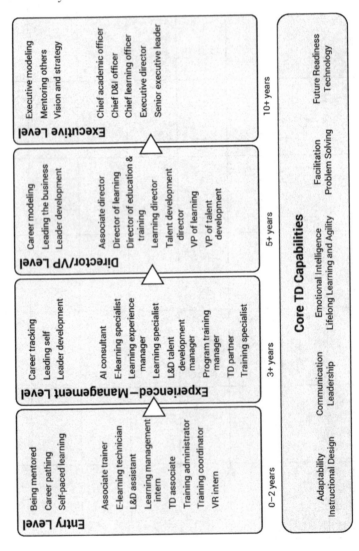

TD Career Adaptability Checklist

Name: _____

This Career Adaptability Checklist is a tool for you or a person you are mentoring. Use this checklist to assist you (or your mentee) in recognizing opportunities to apply adaptability skills on the path to a high AQ. Essential steps are included to remind you about things that may be helpful as you navigate your career landscape. You are able to include additional steps you may identify for yourself along the way. Return to this checklist monthly or quarterly as you see fit. Choose the steps you plan to complete.

❑ Review adaptability methods and processes provided in *Adaptability in Talent Development*: Which methods or processes will I use? How and when?

_____

_____

❑ Complete Adaptability Assessment

❑ Complete a Personal Adaptability Skills Inventory (list those things that make you adaptable)

❑ Set adaptability SMART goals

❑ Start the TD Career Landscape

❑ Select tracking tool (journal or other) to capture daily or weekly application of adaptability skills: collaboration, creativity, curiosity, flexibility, innovation, optimism, risk taking, versatility, others:

_____

_____

❑ Evaluate your support system. Add or remove people as needed by identifying who helps fuel growth.

❑ Determine a planned approach to encouraging, motivating, or supporting others daily, weekly, or on another schedule, and add this to your development plan as a SMART goal.

❑ Identify ways to stay updated on best practices, buzz topics, innovation, and trends in your field (articles, blogs, books, LinkedIn, and others). Add this to your development plan as a SMART goal.

TD Career Adaptability Checklist Continued

❏ Identify barriers or challenges to your adaptability at work, home, or both:

_____

_____

❏ Determine options to overcome barriers or challenges:

_____

_____

❏ Choose frequency to track and evaluate development plan (weekly, monthly, or quarterly).

Other: _____

_____

_____

Other: _____

_____

_____

References

Ang, C. 2020. "Ranked: The 50 Most Innovative Companies." Visual Capitalist, July 17. visualcapitalist.com/top-50-most-innovative-companies-2020.

ASTD (American Society for Training & Development). 2005. *2005 State of the Industry*. Alexandria, VA: American Society for Training & Development.

ATD (Association for Talent Development). 2019. *2019 State of the Industry*. Alexandria, VA: ATD Press.

ATD (Association for Talent Development). 2021. "What Is Talent Development?" Talent Development Glossary Terms. td.org/talent-development-glossary-terms /what-is-talent-development.

Bandura, A. 1977. *Social Learning Theory*. Englewood Cliffs, NJ: Prentice Hall.

Blaschka, A. 2019. "The Number One Soft Skill Employers Seek." *Forbes*, February 28. forbes.com/sites/amyblaschka/2019/02/28/the-number-one-soft-skill-employers -seek-and-five-ways-top-leaders-say-to-cultivate-yours/?sh=644918353d9a.

Bravata, D.M., et al. 2020. "Prevalence, Predictors, and Treatment of Impostor Syndrome: Systematic Review." *Journal of General Internal Medicine* 35(4): 1252–1275.

Chandler, M., et al. 2019. "2019 Global Talent Trends." LinkedIn Talent Solutions. business.linkedin.com/content/dam/me/business/en-us/talent-solutions/resources /pdfs/global-talent-trends-2019.pdf.

Connors, R., T. Smith, and C. Hickman. 2010. *The OZ Principle: Getting Results Through Individual and Organizational Accountability*. New York: Portfolio.

Deloitte Access Economics. 2017. "Soft Skills for Business Success." Deloitte, May. deakinco.com/uploads/Whitepaper/deloitte-au-economics-deakin-soft-skills -business-success-170517.pdf .

Dixon-Fyle, S., K. Dolan, V. Hunt, and S. Prince. 2020. "Diversity Wins: How Inclusion Matters." McKinsey & Company report, May 19. mckinsey.com /featured-insights/diversity-and-inclusion/diversity-wins-how-inclusion-matters.

Duhigg, C. 2012. *The Power of Habit: Why We Do What We Do in Life and Business.* New York: Random House.

Ettling, M. 2015. "How to Attract Talent for Jobs That Don't Exist Yet." *Forbes*, October 13. forbes.com/sites/sap/2015/10/13/how-to-attract-talent-for-jobs-that-dont-yet-exist /?sh=4d08e84c7726.

Godin, S. 2017. "Let's Stop Calling Them 'Soft Skills.'" It's Your Turn, January 31. itsyourturnblog.com/lets-stop-calling-them-soft-skills-9cc27ec09ecb.

Jobs, S. 1994. "Steve Jobs Secrets of Life." Interviewed by Silicon Valley Historical Society. Posted October 6, 2011. youtube.com/watch?v=kYfNvmFoBqw&t=9s.

Lencioni, P. 2002. "Make Your Values Mean Something." *Harvard Business Review*, July. hbr.org/2002/07/make-your-values-mean-something.

LinkedIn Learning. 2020. 2020 *Workplace Learning Report.* LinkedIn Learning. learning.linkedin.com/content/dam/me/learning/resources/pdfs/LinkedIn -Learning-2020-Workplace-Learning-Report.pdf.

Matthews, G. 2015. "Goal Research Summary." Paper presented at the Ninth Annual International Conference of the Psychology Research Unit of Athens Institute for Education and Research (ATINER), Athens, Greece.

Maxwell, J.C. 2017. *No Limits.* New York: Center Street.

Megginson, L. 1963. "Lessons From Europe for American Business." *Southwestern Social Science Quarterly* 44(1): 3–13.

Milenkovic, M. 2019. "42 Worrying Workplace Stress Statistics." American Institute of Stress, Daily Life, September 25. stress.org/42-worrying-workplace-stress-statistics.

Munroe, M. 2020. "Myles Munroe Talk About Eagles | No Fear Of Storms | Mindset of Champion." Video. Eric Skeldon, May 11. youtube.com/watch?v=657Uz09gthg.

Murray, S. 2019. "Is 'AQ' More Important Than Intelligence?" BBC, Worklife 101, November 6. bbc.com/worklife/article/20191106-is-aq-more-important-than -intelligence.

O'Connor, M.J., and T. Alessandra. 1998. *The Platinum Rule: Discover the Four Basic Business Personalities and How They Can Lead You to Success.* New York: Warner Books.

Obama, B., and M. Obama. 2016. "The Final Interview With the Obamas." Interview by S. Sobieraj Westfall and J. Cagle. PEN | People, December 20. youtube.com /watch?v=iH1ZJVqJO3Y&t=1181s.

Risley, J. 2020. "BOPIS Grows More Than 500% During Pandemic." Digital Commerce 360, June 25. digitalcommerce360.com/2020/06/25/bopis-grows-more-than-500 -during-pandemic.

Sinek, S. 2009. *Start With Why: How Great Leaders Inspire Everyone to Take Action*. New York: Portfolio.

Slutsky, I. 2010. "'Chief Listeners' Use Technology to Track, Sort Company Mentions." AdAge, August 30. adage.com/article/digital/marketing-chief-listeners-track -brand-mentions/145618.

Stoltz, P.G. 2000. *Adversity Quotient @ Work: Make Everyday Challenges the Key to Your Success*. New York: William Morrow.

Washington, B.T. 1900. *Up From Slavery: An Autobiography*.

Whiting, K. 2020. "These Are the Top 10 Job Skills of Tomorrow—and How Long it Takes to Learn Them." World Economic Forum, October 21. weforum.org/agenda /2020/10/top-10-work-skills-of-tomorrow-how-long-it-takes-to-learn-them.

World Economic Forum. 2018. *The Future of Jobs Report 2018*. weforum.org/docs/WEF _Future_of_Jobs_2018.pdf.

Yousafzai, M. 2013. "Malala Yousafzai: 16th Birthday Speech at the United Nations." Malala Fund, July 12. malala.org/newsroom/archive/malala-un-speech.

Index

Page numbers followed by *f* refer to figures.

About the Author

Esther Jackson is a project manager, local college instructor, instructional designer, and trainer. She focuses on the evolving learning needs and expectations of today's multigenerational workforce. Esther has a proven track record of equipping people with the skills and knowledge to face challenges in the midst of constant change by addressing the employee experience, workforce engagement, performance, and professional development.

Esther acquired more than 20 years of combined experience in HR leadership, project management, talent development, and diversity and inclusion. Her dedication and commitment to the development, productivity, and performance success of others has helped propel her in multiple roles in the public and private sectors. She has also taken the stage speaking at multiple national and local conferences, in addition to writing articles on talent development and diversity topics.

Esther serves as a national advisor for chapters with the Association for Talent Development (ATD), and has held various roles with the ATD Detroit Chapter, including president.

Esther has a bachelor's and master's degree in education from Wayne State University. She has a doctoral degree in higher education and adult learning from Walden University. Her doctoral study on technology preferences of multiple generations in the workplace classroom has received nearly 1,000 downloads since its publication three years ago. Esther also holds an AQ Foundations Certification from AQai.